This book belongs to

Reece

...a girl who wants to make *really* good choices!

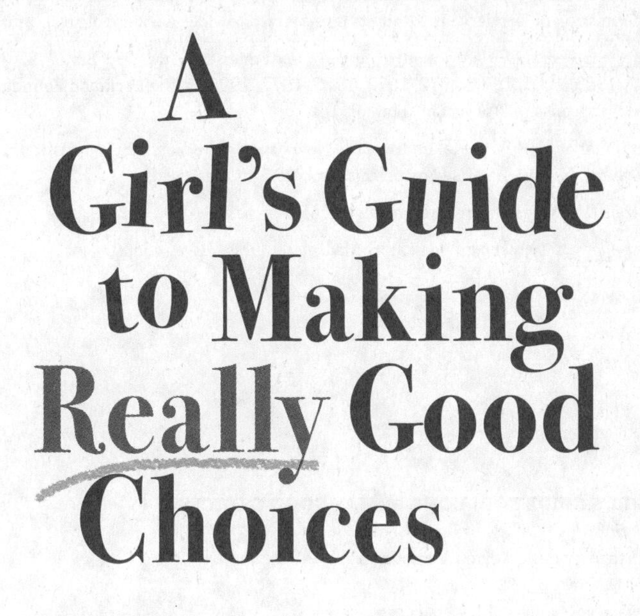

ELIZABETH
GEORGE

Cover by Dugan Design Group, Bloomington, Minnesota

Cover photos © iStockphoto / design56; Monkey Business Images / Shutterstock

A GIRL'S GUIDE TO MAKING REALLY GOOD CHOICES

Published by Harvest House Publishers
Eugene, Oregon 97402
www.harvesthousepublishers.com

Library of Congress Cataloging-in-Publication Data
George, Elizabeth,
A girl's guide to making really good choices / Elizabeth George.
pages cm
ISBN 978-0-7369-5122-7 (pbk.)
ISBN 978-0-7369-5123-4 (eBook)
1. Girls—Conduct of life. 2. Girls—Religious life. 3. Choice (Psychology—Religious aspects—Christianity. 4. Decision making—Religious aspects—Christianity. I. Title.
BJ1651.G46 2013
248.8'2—dc23

2013014353

Printed in the United States of America

14 15 16 17 18 19 20 21 / VP JH / 10 9 8 7 6 5 4

It is with extreme delight that this book
is lovingly dedicated to
my four granddaughters, my "girls":

Taylor Zaengle
Katie Seitz
Grace Seitz
Lily Seitz

It is such a joy to see the four of you
loving God and desiring to make choices
based on His Word. I love you, cherish you,
and pray fervently for you.

Acknowledgments

For Barb Sherrill, vice president of marketing at Harvest House Publishers, a *very* special thank you! I'll never forget our publishing meeting when you poured out your heart, asking for a book for tween girls so the girls you teach in your preteen Sunday school class could have a special book to study, a book just for them. Barb, the result of your passion was my book *A Girl After God's Own Heart*. You knew the need...which has now expanded to a second book, this book—*A Girl's Guide to Making* Really *Good Choices*. I thank you, and I'm sure moms, grandmoms, aunts, and teachers around the globe are joining with me. Thank you for dedicating your time and your heart to the young girls who pass through your class at church.

Contents

1. You Have a Choice 9

2. Choosing to Get Up 23

3. Choosing to Read Your Bible 37

4. Choosing to Pray 51

5. Choosing Your Friends 67

6. Choosing What You Say...and Don't Say . . . 83

7. Choosing to Be Patient 97

8. Choosing a Happy Heart. 111

9. Choosing to Be Faithful 125

10. Choosing to Trust God 139

1

You Have a Choice

Hi there! I'm your new friend, Elizabeth. And I am soooo excited to be talking with you about the many wonderful choices you get to make as a girl after God's own heart. I am really looking forward to being with you as you go through this important book that's just for you.

To help me illustrate some of the many choices you get to make, I will be sharing a few stories from the life of a girl your age named Megan. Her choices, both good and not so good, will give you and me *lots* to talk about.

But before we look at Megan's life and her choices, I want to talk to you for a moment. A great thing about being a girl your age is that you are now able to make some choices about yourself, your attitudes, your habits, your friends, and your hobbies and activities. You are in a fantastic stage of life where you can think, and study, and pray, and talk to others—all of which help you to make the choices God wants you to make about your time, your attitudes, and your activities.

Fun in God's Word!

As we begin putting together a guide for making *really* good choices, you already know that life is full of choices. In fact, you have made a choice to start reading this book! My prayer is that when you are finished, you will see how important your choices are, and how they affect your present daily life as well as your future.

Yes, life is full of choices. Right now there are a lot of people in your life—like your parents and teachers—who are making choices for you. For instance, you have no choice where you live, where you go to school, what you study, and maybe even when you have to go to bed. But whether others make them for you, or you make your own choices, it helps to know what is involved in making *really* good choices.

So let's see what God's Word, the Bible, says about choices. In each chapter, we will look at Bible verses and answer some questions about the important topic covered in the chapter. Our goal is to let God teach us about how to make *really* good choices. So go find your favorite pen or pencil and keep it handy for writing down your answers as you look at verses from the Bible. We are going to spell out **C-H-O-I-C-E-S**.

Choices deal with your heart. There are lots of choices that you and girls like Megan can and will make for yourself. They are choices that deal with your heart, which then affect your attitudes and finally your actions. What do these verses say about your heart attitude?

Above all else, guard your heart, for everything you do flows from it (Proverbs 4:23).

God's command:

guard your choices

Why?

So you make good choices

A good man brings good things out of the good stored up in his heart, and an evil man brings evil things out of the evil stored up in his heart (Luke 6:45).

What happens to the things you store up in your heart?

If the things are good...

you use them

If the things are evil...

you don't use them

There are lots of choices that are left up to you. Do you realize how many choices you make by yourself every day? Being kind to others, especially at home, is your choice. So is deciding whether or not to gossip about another girl. So is choosing to share your things with your brother or sister. And that's making me think of a great choice you could make to help your younger brother or sister get dressed, find their shoes, and get buckled up in the car. And how about the choice to obey Mom and Dad the *first* time they ask you to do something?

On and on goes the long list of choices you get to make all by yourself. So the issue is not whether you are "allowed" to make choices: You *are* already making choices, with or without your parents' input and approval. Wouldn't it be great to have a "guide" to help you know how to make the right choices? Not just good choices, or better choices, but the best choices? Read on!

Having a plan helps you make good choices. Your choices for today started with the plans you made yesterday. For example, *today* you need to decide to set your alarm clock so it goes off *tomorrow* morning. And *today* you have to decide when you need to get up *tomorrow* so you can set your alarm for that time.

Think about what's going on in your life tomorrow. Do you have a class report due? Is your flute lesson after school? Is tomorrow pizza day at school or do you need to take a lunch? And do you need to study for that big test that's coming up next week? And don't forget to ask Mom what else is happening tomorrow so you can add that into your plan.

The plans of the diligent lead to profit (Proverbs 21:5).

What does this bit of Bible wisdom teach you about the value of making plans?

____

Do you want tomorrow to be profitable? Do you want to be successful tomorrow? Are you tired of forgetting to do important things? Then let's work on your plan for tomorrow! List what you know is happening tomorrow so you can start thinking about the choices you will need to make today:

____

____

____

Order your choices with God in mind. I hope before you finish this book you realize how important it is to always be thinking about what *God* wants you to do. God wants to help you make the very best choices. Read on to discover how He helps you do this:

If any of you lacks wisdom, you should ask God...and it will be given to you (James 1:5).

According to this verse, what is the best way to get God's help and direction for the choices you must make?

____

What does God promise to do when you ask Him for wisdom regarding your choices?

____

Every day you have opportunities to make many, many choices. Don't forget to include God in them. When you must make a choice, whisper to God and ask for His help: "God, what is the right thing to do? What do *You* want me to do?"

Influence affects choices. What do I mean by *influence*? When someone or something affects the choices you make, *you are being influenced*.

For example: Have you ever wanted a specific pair of shoes just because your best friend got that very same pair of shoes? Or, do you watch a certain TV show just because it's cool with the other girls at school? That's influence—your choices are shaped by what other people do.

This brings us to another fact about choices: Choices are never made without influence. You may not realize it, but you are constantly being influenced by other people and your feelings when you make your choices. Your family, your friends, and even your own fears and pride have a strong influence on what you choose to do or not do.

Therefore, it is important for you to have people around you who are a good influence on you. Here's what God says:

> *Do not be misled: "Bad company corrupts good character"* (1 Corinthians 15:33).

What happens when you are around the wrong kinds of people?

____

____

What kinds of people should you choose to spend your time with?

____

____

____

Here's something to think about: Do *you* influence others for good or bad?

Choices have one of two results. I'm sure you already know one thing about choices—they always have results. Sometimes those results are good...and sometimes they are not so good! For instance, if you choose to spend all your allowance on candy, then you won't have any money left when you see an awesome pen or bracelet or craft kit. Not having enough money for something useful and lasting—because you blew it on something you ate!—is a consequence of making a choice about the use of your money.

Let's meet one of the women in the Bible who made a choice that still influences us today. You probably already know quite a bit about this woman. Eve was the first woman, the first wife, the first mom...and the first person to sin. The result of her sin is what we now refer to as "the Fall." Here's what the Bible says happened. Get your pen handy and mark away!

> *And the* LORD *God commanded the man, "You are free to eat from any tree in the garden"* (Genesis 2:16).

What did God tell Adam and Eve they could do?

____

____

____

> *"...but you must not eat from the tree of the knowledge of good and evil, for when you eat from it you will certainly die"* (Genesis 2:17).

What did God tell Adam and Eve *not* to do?

____

____

____

What reason did God give Adam and Eve?

____

____

____

When the woman saw that the fruit of the tree was good for food and pleasing to the eye, and also desirable for gaining wisdom, she took some and ate it. She also gave some to her husband, who was with her, and he ate it (Genesis 3:6).

What did Eve do?

____

____

____

Why did Eve do this?

____

____

____

So the LORD God banished him [and Eve] *from the Garden of Eden to work the ground from which he had been taken* (Genesis 3:23).

List two results of Eve's wrong choice.

1. ____

____

2. ____

____

Talk about consequences! Because of Eve's choice to disobey God's specific instructions, sin entered the perfect world God had created. Adam and Eve were sent out of the Garden of Eden and were separated from the presence of God.

Everyone's choices are different. For example, Megan's friend Janice is allowed to make different choices than Megan is. Both of Janice's parents work and Janice is at home alone for some of each day. This gives her more responsibility and more choices than Megan has. This doesn't mean Janice's choices are right or wrong, but they are definitely different from the choices Megan gets to make.

I'm sure you know lots of girls whose parents see things differently from the way your parents do. But you cannot compare your range of choices with those of the other girls you know. However, we do know one thing that God says about the choices you should make when it comes to following the wishes of your parents:

> *Children, obey your parents in the Lord, for this is right* (Ephesians 6:1).

Who is it God wants *you* to obey?

____

The choices other girls are making should not be important to you. What other girls do or don't do is not your standard. Why? Because God has given you *your* parents—to guide *you*. Make this your principle: Your choices should come from standards set by God and the wishes of your parents.

Seeking advice helps you make better choices. Making *really* good choices requires you to ask for advice. The book of Proverbs repeatedly speaks about the foolishness of making choices without seeking the help of others. For instance,

> *The way of fools seems right to them, but the wise listen to advice* (Proverbs 12:15).

In this verse, what word is used to describe people who do not ask for advice?

____

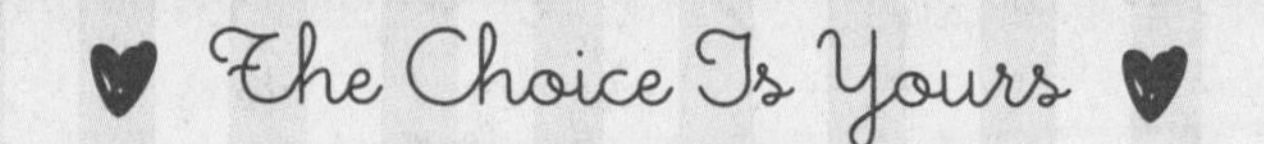

The Choice Is Yours

Every day—and even every minute—you have choices to make. One goal of this book is for you to learn to look at the many choices you *could* make, to consider them all, and then choose one—hopefully a *really* good one, a right one.

Does this sound scary? Well, I have good news for you. In many cases, God tells you exactly what the right choice is. He does this in His Word, the Bible. Sometimes He gives it to you in a command from His Word and actually tells you what the right choice is. In the chapters to come we will look at some choices you get to make—and must make—and see what God says about them!

Making Really Good Choices

In this chapter we have looked into God's Word and learned about why it is important to make really good **C-H-O-I-C-E-S**. On this page, write out the point of each letter as it was stated in your book. (I'll get you started with "C.")

Now, write out one thing you liked, learned, or want to do about the choices you need to make.

____

____

____

____

____

____

Take time now to seal your desire to make really good choices with the words of this prayer:

Dear Father in heaven, thank You that I am growing up and can now make some of my own choices. I have to admit it is a little scary! Help me remember to come to You and ask for Your wisdom so I can make really good choices! Amen.

2

Choosing to Get Up

Megan had a problem. Well, it wasn't a *terribly* big problem in her opinion, or in the grand scheme of the whole universe. But it was causing Megan's life to spin out of control day after day. In short, she was having trouble getting out of bed!

It all started the night before when she had chosen to stay up after her mother firmly told her it was time for bed. Megan loved to read, and she had just been to the library and picked up the next book in her new favorite series. She hadn't intended to stay up, but now she was about to have a really rude awakening.

Can you picture the scene—and the sound? Megan was in a dead sleep. Totally knocked out! And then there was a terrible noise. It took a while for Megan to realize what that sound was—it was her mom speaking to her with her voice raised just loud enough to make her realize she was in deep trouble.

Fun in God's Word!

It's obvious that Megan now wishes she had made a better choice about going to bed. As we work our way through this book about your life and your choices, you'll see this one singular choice—getting up on time—will give direction for the rest of each day. You'll see how Choice #1 (getting up), affects Choice #2...and #3...and #4. Your choices—like getting up or not getting up—create consequences that affect all the events that will come later in your day.

It's time again to look at God's Word, the Bible, and find out what God says about getting to bed...and getting up. Go find a cool pen and write down your answers as we look up some verses from the Bible. We are going to spell out **G-E-T-U-P**.

God's Word talks about being lazy. The Bible has a lot to say about a person who is lazy, calling such a person a "sluggard," or someone who has a bad habit of not wanting to get out of bed, someone who is slow or wants to goof off all day. A sluggard is anyone who hates to get up and hates to work. It's also someone who moves slowly out of laziness—much like the way a giant slug moves slowly across a sidewalk or driveway. Now read Proverbs 6:9-11, and write out the two questions that are asked in the two verses.

How long will you lie there, you sluggard? When will you get up from your sleep? A little sleep, a little slumber, a little folding of the hands to rest—and poverty [ruin] *will come on you like a thief* (Proverbs 6:9-11).

Question #1:

___

___

___

Question #2:

___

___

___

What happens to a sluggard who wants to sleep?

___

___

___

___

A sluggard doesn't even know that he is in trouble, as his ruin comes upon him like a ___________.

Here's another verse about a sluggard:

As a door turns on its hinges, so a sluggard turns on his bed (Proverbs 26:14).

How is a sluggard like a door turning on its hinges, as described in this verse?

____

____

____

____

Evaluate the advantage of getting up. Do you know what the word *evaluate* means? It means to look closely at something. Let's take a closer look at a few Bible characters to see how they responded to a new day. As you go through this section, feel free to mark up and interact with the verses. These people have an important message for you and me! Go ahead and make notes in the margin.

The excellent woman of Proverbs 31—If you read Proverbs 31:10-31, it may remind you of your mom—which is a good thing! These verses make up a Hebrew poem, and each verse highlights a character quality. Guess what habit is described in Proverbs 31, verse 15?

> *She gets up while it is still night; she provides food for her family and portions for her female servants.*

When does this lady get up?

____

____

What is one of the reasons she gets up?

____

____

This lady was a wife and mom, just like your mom. For her to fulfill one of God's priorities for her—to take care of her family—she had to get up and get going really early. Living her life God's way was important enough to get a jump start on the day, and that is true for you too! God has important things for you to do each day. What does this mom teach you about each new day of your life?

____

____

____

The women at the tomb—This loyal group of women also serves as an example for us to follow. They loved Jesus. And when He was dying on the cross, they were with Him to the very end. Then they followed those who carried their Savior's body to see where He was buried. And once they got home, they did the work of preparing spices for Jesus' body so He could be properly buried. Read on to find out what happened next when the Sabbath was over.

> *...very early in the morning, the women took the spices they had prepared and went to the tomb* (Luke 24:1).

What did the women do?

____

____

____

When did this happen?

____

____

Do you think these women were tired? Do you think it was horrible watching Jesus suffer brutality and die in agony on the cross? And yet they pressed on with their mission—to tend to Jesus' body and burial. What if they had turned on their hinges on their beds during that all-important morning when they needed to minister to the Lord? What if they had made excuses? What if they had decided they were just too tired? What if they had slept in?

Stop here and write a few words about why it is important for you to get up in the morning.

____

____

Jesus—Jesus teaches us about an important habit in His life:

Very early in the morning, while it was still dark, Jesus got up, left the house and went off to a solitary place, where he prayed (Mark 1:35).

What was Jesus' goal in this verse?

____

____

Where did He do this?

____

____

And when did He do this?

____

____

Jesus talked to His heavenly Father first thing in the morning. He prayed to God. He received daily strength for doing God's will for one more day. He was armed for facing and handling all kinds of temptation, especially the temptation to turn away from going to the cross.

Tweens who get up. What young girl doesn't dream of being a gymnast? Did you watch the gymnastics or swimming competitions during the last Olympics? Many of those girls were young—they were just a few years older than you. To get to the Olympics, they had to get up early before school to train at the gym or at a swimming pool to become some of the world's greatest athletes.

What about those who have animals? I have a friend whose daughter has a horse. She gets up very early while it is still dark to feed and brush her horse before school. My niece was on an ice-skating team. Guess what time she had to be at the ice rink for practice in the morning? Five o'clock—every weekday. Then she was off to school.

If you want to become good at any sport or playing an instrument or doing anything else, it starts with getting up in the morning. What is it you are passionate about? What is it you love doing more than anything else? What is it you like doing but never seem to have enough time for? Take a minute to jot down an answer or two—a dream or two! Then tell how getting up might help you fulfill your desires.

____

____

____

____

Understand the importance of getting up. Are you looking for a good day with time for not only the necessary stuff, but also for some fun stuff too? Then there's one *really simple* but *really hard* choice you've got to make every day. In fact, it is the first choice—and a *really* good one—you must make every day, whether you realize it or not. That choice is, will you get up when you need to...or not?

What does this verse say about doing things right?

Everything should be done in a fitting and orderly way (1 Corinthians 14:40).

____

____

When you don't get outta that bed when you're supposed to so you can get everything done in a "fitting and orderly way," *every*thing suffers for the rest of the day. It is amazing how that one first choice influences everything else.

Purpose to get up. As you think about living your life God's way, let the following choices pave the path for a better tomorrow. This exercise will help you follow through on your first step toward a better life—getting out of bed!

Step 1: Decide with your parents when you should get up. Yes, your parents will wonder if you are okay when you ask for their help, but do it anyway. When is a good time to talk with them about this?

____

Step 2: Determine when you need to get up to make your day go the way you want it to go. The best time for me to get up is ______________.

Step 3: Set your alarm...a good *loud* one. An obnoxious one!

Step 4: Get to bed in time to get the rest you need *before* getting-up time. (No all-night reading marathons allowed!)

Step 5: Pray. Ask for God's help to get up at the right time. Tell Him about your plans, commitments, and dreams for tomorrow. Go ahead. He cares!

Step 6: Purpose to get up...no matter what. Just for one morning, don't give in to the temptation to snooze or turn over to sleep some more. And don't worry about not getting enough sleep for that day. It's only for *one* morning!

Step 7: Praise God when you hear the alarm. Read Psalm 118:24 below, and then write out from Psalm 118:24 what the psalmist cried out with the new day, then make it your cry too.

The LORD has done it this very day; let us rejoice today and be glad.

____

____

____

____

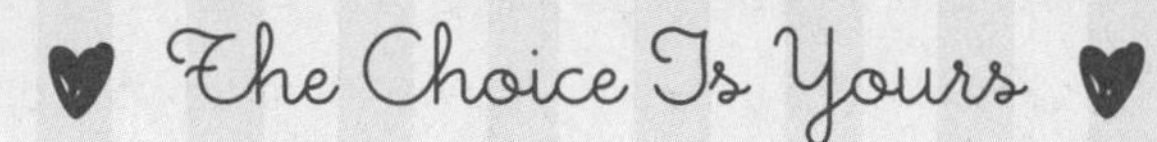

The Choice Is Yours

I like to do things in small steps. It is so much easier that way. And it makes success more achievable. So instead of saying, "I'm going to choose to get up on time or early every day for the rest of my life," I try to get up on time for just one day. You see, who you are today is who you have been becoming. And who you are today is who you will be in the future...if nothing changes.

Every choice you repeat—either good or bad—is creating the real you, who you really are. Each choice—whether good or bad—made over and over again becomes a habit. And your goal (like mine) is to make the *really* good choices over and over again until you've established good habits, godly habits.

My friend, your life is a precious gift from God. On top of the life He has given you, He also has incredible plans for you. Nothing could be worse than a life that counts for nothing. But God gives you all the opportunities in the world to make a difference, to help others, and to honor Him.

Each morning when your sleep is shattered by the sound of your alarm, realize that it is right then and right there that you make maybe *the* most important choice you'll make all day. It goes like this. If you get up, you are in control of yourself and your day. (Well, at least you're in control of how it begins!)

Why can I say this? Because from Minute #1, you are calling the shots. You are in the driver's seat of your day, so to speak, when you make a choice to get up. You've at least started your day down the right path. And what a great day it will be!

Making Really Good Choices

In this chapter we have looked into God's Word and learned how important it is to **G-E-T-U-P**. On this page write out the point of each letter. (I'll get you started with "G.")

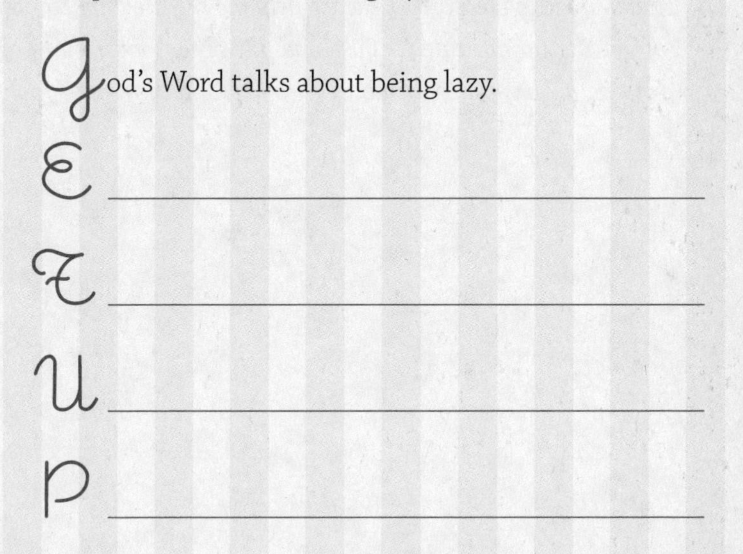

Now write out one thing you liked, learned, or want to do about getting up.

Take time now to seal your desire to make *really* good choices with the words of this prayer:

Dear Jesus, I have so much I want to do with my life. I especially want to please You. Please help me see the importance of getting up on time for just one day. Then, with more of Your help, I'll get up on time for the next, and the next! Amen.

3

Choosing to Read Your Bible

As she wipes the sleep from her eyes, Megan tells herself, "Quick, think fast!" But it's too late. Her mother barges into her room with a very irritated look and asks, "Why aren't you up and dressed? You've got school today!"

With a fresh idea in her mind, Megan blurts out, "There must be something wrong with my alarm clock! It didn't go off." (Yeah, let's blame it on the alarm clock!) "You know, Mom, you really need to buy me a new one."

And, for her final argument, Megan pleads, "Why didn't you wake me up, Mom? You knew I have a big day at school today!"

With this final round of words filled with blame, Megan's mom raises up her hands in exasperation and walks out of the room. Before she steps out, she looks over her shoulder and says, "Hurry up for breakfast before we are all late!"

As Megan staggers out of bed, she notices her Bible lying on the nightstand along with the study book her Sunday school class is going through. "Oh no! I didn't finish today's lesson." Megan lets out a sigh, "Oh well, no big deal.

Right now I've got more important things to deal with. I'm late for school! Maybe I can finish my Bible lesson during lunch break."

Fun in God's Word!

Are you remembering Choice #1, the one that starts the day off right? If you are still in the dark, look again at chapter 2 and write the title here:

____

Each morning when your sleep is shattered like Megan's was, realize that it is right then and right there that you make what may be *the* most important choice you'll make all day. It goes like this. If you get up right away, you are in control of yourself and your day. (Well, at least you're in control of how it begins! You have to leave room for God's plan, for interruptions, and even for crises.)

Now it's time for another choice: Choice #2 is *to spend time with God*—to have a quiet time. This is where God "speaks" to you through His Word and gives you the plan for your day. This choice to meet with God will set the tone of your day...and your voice...and your words...and your actions...and your attitudes...and the way you treat people—starting right at home! So once you're up, you want to make God your #1 priority. You want to choose to put first things first. You want to meet with Him before the day gets rolling.

It's time again to look at God's Word, the Bible, and find

out what God says about choosing to read your Bible. With your trusty pen, write down your answers as we look up some verses. We are going to spell out **B-I-B-L-E**.

Bible reading is a must. A *priority* is something seen as important, something you put at the top of your to-do list every day. Why should reading the Bible be a priority? Because that is where you find out more about God, who *should* be your #1 priority, right? A great place to start learning about God is Genesis 1:1:

In the beginning God created the heavens and the earth.

This is the very first verse of the Bible. What does it tell you about God?

____

____

After you get out of bed, you want to make the really good choice to spend time in the Bible. It's a key time for learning about the God who created you and everything around you.

Important answers come from the Bible. I'm sure that at your age, you are beginning to have a lot of questions about life. Read the questions below and check the ones you would like to have answered.

_____ Are you wondering about your future?

_____ Are you looking for a few good friends?

_____ Are you tired of doing the wrong thing?

_____ Would you like to get along better with your parents?

Well, I've got great news for you! Time in God's Word will help you to have success in every one of these areas—and more. You can learn this from looking at a man in the Bible whose name is Joshua. He was the man who took Moses' place when Moses died, and he became the general of God's army.

Like every general and leader—and every follower of God—Joshua wondered if he would be successful in living out God's will. God's assignment for Joshua was to win the battle to gain the Promised Land for God's people.

Of course, God's assignment for you will be different, but like Joshua, you will want to be successful when you carry out God's plan. Read the verse below and write out the command God gave Joshua to guarantee his success.

> *Be careful to obey all the law* [the Bible] *my servant Moses gave you...that you may be successful wherever you go* (Joshua 1:7).

____

____

____

____

Now read the next verse and write out the two things God told Joshua to do to make sure he would be successful in God's eyes.

Keep this Book of the Law always on your lips; meditate on it day and night...Then you will be prosperous and successful (Joshua 1:8).

1. ____

____

2. ____

____

God wants to bless you and help you have success. Are you wondering what you can do to help make this success happen? Here are a few steps you can take each day, steps that will help you choose God as a top priority—actually, your #1 priority!

Step 1: Read your Bible. I could say, "Just read it!" Start anywhere you like. You could even start with the book of Joshua! The only wrong way to read the Bible is not to read the Bible.

Step 2: Study your Bible. Ask your parents or youth leader to help you find some simple ways to get to know your Bible better.

Step 3: Hear the Bible taught. Make sure you go to your youth group meetings and to church to hear God's Word taught and explained so you can understand it. And, of course, choose to do what it says!

Step 4: Memorize verses from the Bible. God told Joshua to "meditate" on the Bible. That means to think about God's Word a lot and memorize it so it is always in your heart.

Step 5: Desire to spend time in God's Word. You already know how important it is to eat. Well, you need to see the spiritual food the Bible gives you as being even more important than eating physical food. As Job declared, *I have treasured the words of* [God's] *mouth more than my daily bread* (Job 23:12).

Bible truths give you direction. Have you ever gotten lost temporarily in a shopping mall or large store? You looked around and couldn't see your mom or dad or big sister or brother. Being lost is a scary experience. Wouldn't it be nice to always know where you are going and never get lost? How is the Bible described in this verse?

> *Your word* [the Bible] *is a lamp for my feet, a light on my path* (Psalm 119:105).

1. The Bible is ________________________________

____

____

2. The Bible is ______________________________

____

The Bible is like a flashlight that shows you the path your life *should* take—the path God wants you to take. Without that light you could easily stumble and fall—or go down the wrong path spiritually.

As you read the verse that follows, what is a very important goal you should have for your life?

How can a young person stay on the path of purity? (Psalm 119:9).

____

____

Now read the second part of Psalm 119:9. Here God gives you the answer to the question above. Be sure to write out the answer!

By living according to your word [the Bible].

____

____

Are you ready for another cool verse about God and His Word? Read on!

All Scripture [the Bible] *is God-breathed and is useful for teaching, rebuking, correcting and training in righteousness* (2 Timothy 3:16).

What two truths do you learn about the Bible?

1. The Bible is ______________________________

____

2. The Bible is ______________________________

____

Look again at the verse above, 2 Timothy 3:16. Then fill in the blanks below to make a list of the four things the Bible will do to you as you read it:

1. The Bible will ________________________ me.
2. The Bible will ________________________ me.
3. The Bible will ________________________ me.
4. The Bible will ________________________ me.

Which one of the four stands out to you? Circle it as a reminder to do something to grow in this area.

Life changes come from the Bible. You wouldn't want to stay a tween forever, would you? You are looking forward to being a teenager. Here's the good news—you can start making changes to prepare yourself for those years *today!*

Read the two verses below to see what meeting with God in the Bible can do to get you ready for your day—and your life! *Circle* the words that describe God's Word. Then *underline* the effect it has on those who read it. I'll guide you through the first example. Then you can do the other verses yourself.

Psalm 19:7: *The law of the LORD is perfect, refreshing the soul.*

Now try it yourself!

The statutes of the LORD are trustworthy, making wise the simple.

Psalm 19:8: *The precepts of the LORD are right, giving joy to the heart.*

The commands of the LORD are radiant, giving light to the eyes.

Read Psalm 19:10 below and write out how valuable the teaching in the Bible should be.

They are more precious than gold, than much pure gold.

They are sweeter than honey, than honey from the honeycomb.

____

____

____

____

Eternal life is found in the Bible. Have you read anything about the adventures of Ponce de León? He was an explorer who went searching for what was called the Fountain of Youth. He thought if he could find this special fountain and drink some of its water, it would give him eternal youth, eternal life. He would be forever young, and live forever.

You probably don't want to think about staying young forever. But you would probably like to live forever, right? The Bible tells us how that is possible—how you can live forever with Jesus in heaven.

There was a young man in the Bible who wanted to know how to live with Jesus forever. His name was Timothy. Read 2 Timothy 3:15:

> *The Holy Scriptures* [the Bible]...*are able to make you wise for salvation through faith in Christ Jesus.*

What book gave Timothy the wisdom he needed for salvation—for a relationship with Jesus that lasts forever?

___

___

According to this verse, how do we receive salvation?

___

___

Do you want to live with Jesus in heaven and have eternal life? I'm thinking you do! God wants to give you eternal life, but there is just one problem: You need to be perfect, without sin.

Yes, you already know you don't always make the right choices, which leads to doing the wrong things. That is why you need a Savior.

Jesus is perfect. He is God. He is sinless. And He came to earth to die for your sins and be your Savior. Because of Jesus, you can have your sins forgiven and go to heaven.

Choose to believe in the truths about Jesus, God's Son. Then ask God to open your heart to believe in Him.

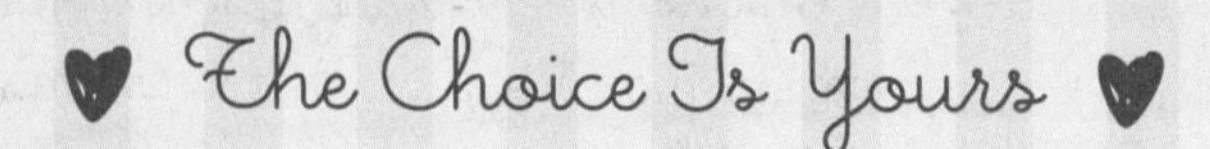

The Choice Is Yours

Sometimes you may think you are just too busy to stop and spend time with God. You have people to see, places to go, and things to do! But trust me, it's worth making the time to spend with God every day! The Bible is a special book. In fact, it is the greatest book ever written. And it is the book that can show you the right way to live for God each day and lead you to eternal life.

And if you are a Christian—if you believe in Jesus and have received Him into your heart as your Savior—you have eternal life. As a Christian, you have God's Spirit in you, the Holy Spirit. He will help guide you as you read God's Word. That's why it is so important for you to choose to spend time reading the Bible. When you read it, you will think differently. You will live differently. You will grow spiritually. And you will be blessed.

Don't you think these blessings are worth the choice to get up a few minutes earlier each day so you can get into God's Word and get His help and guidance for the day ahead? Through the Bible, God will tell you what *really* good choices you need to make. He will show you how to live your life His way.

Making Really Good Choices

In this chapter you have looked into God's Word and learned how important it is to read your **B-I-B-L-E**. On this page, write out the point of each letter. (I'll get you started with "B.")

Now write out one thing you liked, learned, or want to do about getting up and getting into God's Word, the Bible.

Take time now to seal your desire to make really good choices with the words of this prayer:

Hear my prayer, Father. Thank You that Your Word tells me how to live my life and how to make really good choices. And thank You most of all that the Bible shows me Your Son and how He wants me to live for Him here on earth and with Him forever in heaven. Thank You! Amen.

4

Choosing to Pray

"No no no no no! I can't believe I did that! What was I thinking when I signed Miss Julie's 'My Commitment to Pray' card at Sunday school?" muttered Megan. "Everything is going just great in my life. So why do I need to pray? And for who...and what? Missionaries I don't know? Sick people? And sure, family's important, but *puh*-lease don't even talk to me about praying for Bret and Heather. Even though they're my brother and sister, they are such a pain! What a waste of time."

Megan's list of excuses grows longer and longer as she lingers by her bed with a choice to make. She is already running late. And there she stands, trying to justify why she is continuing to fail miserably in fulfilling her commitment to pray every day this week.

Looking back, Megan admits she hadn't really wanted to make this commitment, but the girls in her Sunday school class did. They had loved their teacher's challenge to pray every day for one week. Miss Julie was teaching about prayer and wanted the girls to put into practice what they were learning by making a pledge to pray.

"Oh well, okay. Here goes: 'God, bless the missionaries and my family today, even Bret and Heather (ugh!)—and of course, bless me! Amen.'"

Fun in God's Word!

Poor Megan. She has a lot to learn about prayer, which is simply talking to God. And she didn't know enough of God's Word to realize the power of the many promises God has made to His people. Yes, Megan needed to discover the truth that God hears and answers prayers—even hers.

Does any of this sound familiar? Like Megan, do you think prayer doesn't make any difference, so you aren't too excited about giving it a try? Or, again like our girl Megan, do you think you don't have time to pray, that prayer is a waste of time?

Well, a quick look at God's Word, the Bible, will show you what God says about talking to Him through prayer. Is your pen handy? If not, it's time to go find it so you can write down your answers as we look at some key verses from the Bible. We are going to spell out **P-R-A-Y-E-R**.

Prayer is talking to God. You have no problem talking with your friends, do you? Even during church and Sunday school class it's hard to stop talking. Megan and her best friend, Ginny, could talk nonstop for hours about crafts, or soccer, or the latest book they were reading—and they do! But to talk to someone outside their circle? No way!

It's the same way when it comes to talking to God. When

your relationship with God is not very close, you will find it harder to talk to Him. You won't know what to say, and you won't feel close to Him or comfortable in His presence. What's the solution? Read on to see what these verses say you need to do to get closer to God.

Draw near to God with a sincere heart (Hebrews 10:22).

What is it *you* are to do?

___

What should your heart attitude be when you pray?

___

Come near to God and he will come near to you (James 4:8).

What is your role in prayer?

___

___

What is God's response?

___

___

Be sure to notice that these verses are telling you that it is your responsibility to move toward God. If God feels like a stranger to you, remember, it is *you* who has moved away from God. God did not move away from you.

Try this exercise for one week. Each day just talk to God. "Draw near" and "come near" to Him. Take a step toward God and reach out to Him through prayer. Next, use your pen or pencil to color in the boxes below. Tell God about your worries, questions, and problems. You'll be glad you did. And, of course, you will want to keep doing this day after day!

Today I Talked to God in Prayer						
Monday	Tuesday	Wednesday	Thursday	Friday	Saturday	Sunday

Realize you must pray with a heart of faith. Many Christians have trouble believing in the power of prayer. That was Megan's problem. And like her, we also say, "What difference does prayer make anyway?" We think these thoughts because we don't know the wonderful promises God has made to us about prayer and answering our prayers. As a result, we don't think prayer makes any difference. So...we don't pray.

The Bible has a lot to say about how you should pray. Read on and jot down some answers. Learn all you can about prayer and about talking things over with God.

> *Let us then approach God's throne of grace with confidence, so that we may receive mercy and find grace to help us in our time of need* (Hebrews 4:16).

What is your job in prayer?

____

____

____

What does God give you when you pray?

____

____

____

Whatever you ask for in prayer, believe that you have received it, and it will be yours (Mark 11:24).

What is your job or part in prayer?

1. ____

____

2. ____

____

What does the verse above say happens as a result?

____

____

Think about it: Does this mean you can ask and get anything you want, like a new bike, or a craft kit, or an electronic game? For help with the answer, look at the next verse:

When you ask, you do not receive, because you ask with wrong motives, that you may spend what you get on your pleasures (James 4:3).

What is one huge reason you don't always get what you ask for from God? Underline your answer in the verse above.

Assurances and promises about prayer. It's a fact: We are often clueless about how prayer works. And we don't understand how prayer helps us make *really* good choices. It is probably because we don't really think about how much God loves us. We don't realize that He has the power to guide us and make our lives better.

Now work your way through the Bible verses below, write out from each verse what God is promising to you when you pray:

Ask and it will be given to you; seek and you will find; knock and the door will be opened to you (Matthew 7:7).

Circle the three words that tell you what you are to do when you pray. Don't forget to notice all God will do!

Call to me and I will answer you and tell you great and unsearchable things you do not know (Jeremiah 33:3).

What is it *you* are to do?

____

What is God's promise to you?

____

____

____

If any of you lacks wisdom, you should ask God...and it will be given to you (James 1:5).

God's promise to me is

____

____

You need to confess sin before you pray. Here is another big reason you and lots of other people don't pray: It is because you know you have done something wrong. In your heart you know you need to talk to God about it. You know you need to confess it, to agree with Him that what you did was wrong. But that's a scary thing to do! Take a look at a few verses that talk about confessing your sin.

If I regard [sin] *in my heart, the Lord will not hear* (Psalm 66:18 NKJV).

What happens when you sin and don't confess it to God?

____

____

____

If we confess our sins, he is faithful and just and will forgive us our sins and purify us from all unrighteousness (1 John 1:9).

What happens when you confess your sin and admit it to God?

____

____

Here's a good exercise for dealing with your sins and failures: Make a choice to keep "a short account" with God. This means you deal with any sin instantly, as soon as it occurs—on the spot—at the exact minute that you slip up and fail. Say, "Lord, I'm sorry for ________________. That was wrong. Thank You for forgiving me in Jesus."

Examples of people who prayed. Prayer is an important part of every Christian's life. And the Bible is filled with people who made the *really* good choice to pray about their life and their choices. See what you can learn about the difference that prayer made in these people's lives. Also pay attention to what they talked to God about.

Hannah—Hannah was a woman with a big problem. She wasn't able to have a baby, even though she wanted one desperately. This was Hannah's Problem #1. But Hannah had another problem.

> *Her rival* [a woman named Peninnah] *kept provoking* [Hannah] *in order to irritate her. This went on year after year* (1 Samuel 1:6-7).

What was Hannah's Problem #2?

____

____

> *In her deep anguish Hannah prayed to the LORD...*[saying] *"I have been praying...out of my great anguish and grief"* (1 Samuel 1:10 and 16).

What was Hannah's solution to her problems?

____

____

____

Problems and bullies and mean girls are a fact of life. But the habit of praying to God about your troubles and telling Him all about them will see you through.

Mary—Mary was another woman who prayed. She praised God in prayer! Mary was about 14 years old when she prayed a remarkable prayer of praise to God that Jesus would at last make His appearance on earth—and that *she* would be His mother! This prayer of praise in Luke 1:46-55 is often referred to as "Mary's Song." In the verses that follow, underline what she praised God for.

> *My soul glorifies the Lord and my spirit rejoices in God my Savior ...for the Mighty One has done great things for me—holy is his name. His mercy extends to those who fear him* (verses 46-50).

Now make a check mark in the blank after you offer your own praise to God.

Is God your Savior? Then praise Him. _________

Has God done any great things for you? Then remember a few of them and praise Him. _________

Is God holy and merciful? Then praise Him. _________

Jesus—Jesus was perfect and knew everything about prayer! Read these Bible verses and note what they tell you about His habit of prayer and some of the things He prayed about:

Mark 1:35: *Very early in the morning, while it was still dark, Jesus got up, left the house and went off to a solitary place, where he prayed.*

When did Jesus choose to pray, and where?

____

____

____

John 6:11: *Jesus then took the loaves, gave thanks, and distributed to those who were seated...He did the same with the fish.*

For what did Jesus give thanks?

____

Luke 23:34: *Jesus said, "Father, forgive them, for they do not know what they are doing."*

What did Jesus ask His Father to do?

____

____

Realize that God is always available to you. Have you ever noticed that your parents' cell phones are always on and available? This means people can call them at all hours of the day or night.

Your prayer life is like a cell phone—you can pray anytime you want, anywhere you are, and talk to God for as long as you want. You have a direct line to the God of the universe 24 hours a day, 7 days a week. How's that for immediate access to God? Notice what the following verses say about God's availability.

The LORD is near to all who call on him, to all who call on him in truth (Psalm 145:18).

What do you learn about God in this verse?

____

____

____

What is it you are to do?

____

____

____

And speaking of cell phones, don't forget what God says in Jeremiah 33:3: *Call...me and I will answer you.*

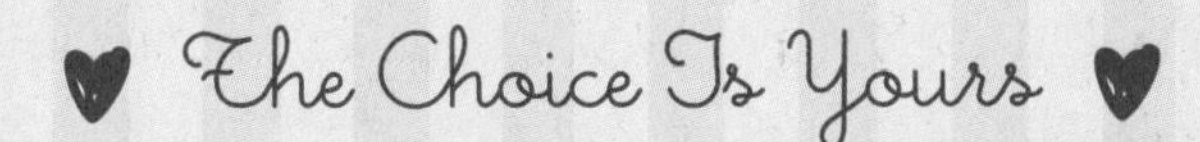

The Choice Is Yours

There are many excuses you can give about why you choose not to pray. You can be like Megan, who chose not to take the time or make an effort to pray. Prayer was simply not a priority for her. It was not important to her. Instead, Megan filled her time with things that she wanted to do—things she thought were more important.

The choice to pray—or not to pray—is yours. You can choose to be like Megan and be so busy you don't even get around to *thinking* about praying. Many girls simply won't do what it takes to talk to God. Prayer is an act of the will. It is a choice. You have to *want* to do it... and *choose* to do it. The choice is yours.

Making Really Good Choices

In this chapter we have looked into God's Word and learned how important **P-R-A-Y-E-R** is. On this page, write out the point of each letter. (I'll get you started with "P.")

Prayer is talking to God.

R______________________________

A______________________________

Y______________________________

E______________________________

R______________________________

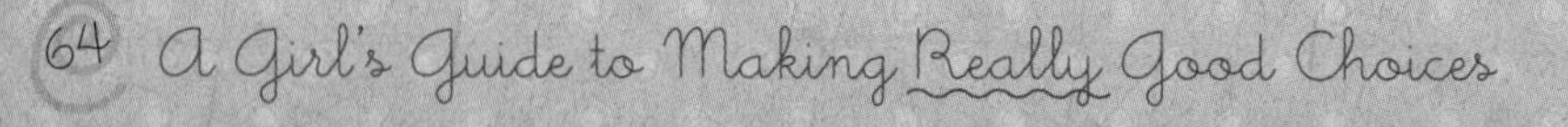

Now write out one thing you liked, learned, or want to do about making prayer an important part of your life.

____

____

____

____

____

____

Take time now to seal your desire to make *really* good choices with the words of this prayer:

Hello, God! This is ________________. I truly want to come closer to You, and talk to You, and know You better. Thank You that I can talk to You anytime from anywhere about anything, and You will hear me. Thanks for being available when I need a friend—a best friend! Amen.

5

Choosing Your Friends

Megan has finally arrived at school. She wasn't sure she would make it after her early morning ordeal at home, but here she was. Being at school wasn't the thing that excited her the most—no, it was her friends!

As Megan makes her way through the hallway to her locker, she runs into some of the girls from church, including her longtime friend, Sarah. Megan likes these girls, and they seem to like her too. But there's just one problem—they aren't very popular at school. They dress a little differently and act differently from the other kids.

As the church girls turn to go to class, Sarah says, "See you Sunday, Meg!" Megan gives them all an embarrassed half smile and half wave. She is in real turmoil. Why? Because part of her wishes she could be stronger in her commitment to Jesus like these girls are. But at the same time, she doesn't want to stand out or be marked as different or weird at school and with her other friends. And that's the problem: The church girls are viewed by the "in group" as "religious weirdos."

Megan turns around just in time to greet Bella, one of the cool girls from the "in crowd" as she walks by on her way to class. Bella is so pretty, and she always wears the latest fashions. Megan has been trying for a long time to be accepted into Bella's group. Hmmm—maybe if Megan helps Bella with her math lesson, Bella will help her become part of her group.

Fun in God's Word!

You may be one of those girls who never meets a stranger. Maybe you have no problem talking to other people—about anything—and you make friends super easily. Or maybe you have a forever childhood friend like Sarah, and the two of you are inseparable. When you get together, you can talk forever! But for a lot of girls, it's not easy to find or make a good friend.

Friends are important. And God knows that. In fact, He gives you guidelines and principles for choosing your friends. Your goal is not to have just any friends, but to have the *right kind* of friends. So with pen in hand, let's go on a treasure hunt in God's Word to discover what He says about friends. We are even going to spell out the word **F-R-I-E-N-D-S**.

Finding a friend takes time. You have probably heard sad tales of girls who don't have any friends. Maybe you feel like that sometimes. But did you know that if you are a Christian, you already have a very special friend in

Jesus? Jesus said to His disciples, *You are my friends...I have called you friends* (John 15:14-15).

With Jesus as your friend, you have the very best friend a person could have. You can talk to Him through prayer about anything, at any time, and in any situation. And best of all, He is always with you. What do the following verses tell you about your friend, Jesus?

Surely I am with you always, to the very end of the age (Matthew 28:20).

Jesus is ____

____

Never will I leave you; never will I forsake you (Hebrews 13:5).

Jesus will ____

____

This is awesome news! Jesus is always with you and available to you. And God also provides others who can and should be your friends. For instance:

You have friends in your parents. Now before you wonder how that is possible, realize that there is nothing weird about being friends with your mom and your dad. The truth is, they are God's gift to you. And no one loves you more or cares about you more than your parents do. Ask God to help you develop a forever friendship with your parents.

You also have friends in your brothers and sisters. You are probably thinking, "Are you kidding? Friends with my loser of a brother? No way!" Or, "Friends with my little sister? Gross! What a headache!"

Believe it or not, your friends throughout life will come and go. You might stay in touch with some, but eventually most of your friends will move on. But your family will always be there, no matter what and no matter where. And here's some good news: Your brother won't always be a loser, and your sister won't always be a headache.

Reject certain people as friends. The Bible is specific about the kind of person to look for as a friend—and the kind to avoid. Here's a list of people God tells you to reject as friends.

> *Walk with the wise and become wise, for a companion of fools suffers harm* (Proverbs 13:20).

A wise friend causes me to...

____

____

A foolish friend causes me to...

____

____

____

Do not make friends with a hot-tempered person, do not associate with one easily angered (Proverbs 22:24).

I am not to be friends with...

___

___

I am not to be friends with...

___

___

Do not be misled: "Bad company corrupts good character" (1 Corinthians 15:33).

What effect does the wrong kind of friend have on you?

___

___

___

Involve your parents. Are you wondering why you should listen to your mom and dad when it comes to your friendships? How could your parents possibly be helpful in your search for good friends?

First, your parents have a little more experience in finding friends than you do. They can be a great help!

And besides, according to God's plan in Ephesians 6:1 (*Children, obey your parents in the Lord, for this is right*), they are the final authority on who you do and don't have as friends.

Take Megan, for example. Megan wanted to be friends with Bella not because Bella was a good and godly influence on her, but because Bella was popular. Megan's parents could see how Bella was influencing Megan in a bad way, which Megan could not even see—or didn't want to see.

Talk to your parents about what kinds of friends and friendships you should have. And be sure your new friends come to your house and meet your parents. You will be glad you did this.

Read 2 Timothy 2:22, which is another "friendship verse":

Flee the evil desires of youth and pursue righteousness, faith, love and peace, along with those who call on the Lord out of a pure heart.

What does this verse say you are to "flee" or run away from?

____

____

____

____

Instead, what should you "pursue" or follow after?

What kinds of friends do you want to have as you grow to be a girl, teen, and woman after God's own heart?

Oh, one final reminder...again: What does the Bible say you should do if your parents say *no* to certain girls being your close friends?

Children, obey your parents in the Lord, for this is right (Ephesians 6:1).

Encourage your friends. Have you ever thought about how easy it is to tell other kids all the things you think they are doing wrong? They are wearing the wrong clothes, or talking funny, or acting weird. Instead of discouraging others, however, what does the Bible say you are to do?

Encourage one another and build each other up (1 Thessalonians 5:11).

____

____

____

Make it a habit to mention the good qualities and attitudes you see in others.

What is the best way to be an encourager? Well, the Bible tells us how Jonathan encouraged his best friend, David. Their friendship was based on their shared love for God. When Jonathan's father, King Saul, wanted to kill David, what did Jonathan do to encourage David?

Saul's son Jonathan went to David...and helped him find strength in God (1 Samuel 23:16).

____

____

____

The best way to encourage your friends is to help them "find strength in God" through the Bible and through prayer. And you can also give compliments. Praise them, not for their cool clothes or things, but for something you appreciate about them, something you admire about their conduct or their character. For example, is your friend honest? Is she committed to the team and faithful? Is she kind and helpful to her little brother or sister? Tell her. When you build up another person instead of tearing her down, you help her grow and develop in a good way. Plus, *you* are being a very good friend!

Nice is always in. Have you ever heard of the Golden Rule? And did you know that Jesus was the one who taught us this rule? Read the Golden Rule below, and write out what Jesus says you are to do to others.

Do to others as you would have them do to you (Luke 6:31).

____

____

____

____

Here's an exercise: List two or three ways you want others to treat you:

____

____

____

____

Now read the Golden Rule again (see Luke 6:31 on the previous page). According to it, how should you be treating others?

____

____

____

____

And remember, the Golden Rule doesn't just say to be nice. Read the next verse. Instead of just being "nice," what does the Bible say you are to do?

Be kind and compassionate to one another (Ephesians 4:32).

____

____

____

____

Here's a bonus activity: The Golden Rule begins at home, because the person you are at home is the person you really are. Write down one way you will practice the Golden Rule this week with your parents and brothers and sisters.

____

____

____

Decide to be yourself. Don't work at impressing others by saying and doing things you think will make them like you. It's tempting to act in a way that goes against God's Word to get friends or be accepted by the "in crowd." What you are looking for in a friend is a girl who isn't fake—someone who is pretending to be the kind of person she is not. For yourself, you should want to be the real thing, to be what God desires you to be—a godly young woman, to be His girl. So be that person, even if it means you won't be the most popular gal at school. At least you will be *you*. You will be genuine, and God will be pleased with you. After all, He made you just the way you are.

Spiritual maturity is important. So choose to be growing spiritually. This applies to your friendships too: If you desire to grow spiritually and know more about God and how He wants you to act, you will want friends who share your desire to grow.

Take a look in the Bible at the young man Daniel. He had three really good young friends who stood with him. Their names were Shadrach, Meshach, and Abednego (Daniel 1:6-7).

God had told the Jewish people they were not allowed to eat certain foods. When the king of Babylon gave Daniel and his three friends some food that was against God's law, they stood strong together and refused to eat the food and asked for only vegetables and water. Read what happened after they chose to eat only what God approved. Then write out the results:

At the end of the ten days they looked healthier and better nourished than any of the young men who ate the royal food (Daniel 1:15).

____

____

____

Are you wondering where you will find friends who will stay strong when it comes to doing what the Bible says, what God says? Here's a hint—you'll usually find these girlfriends at church or in a Sunday school class!

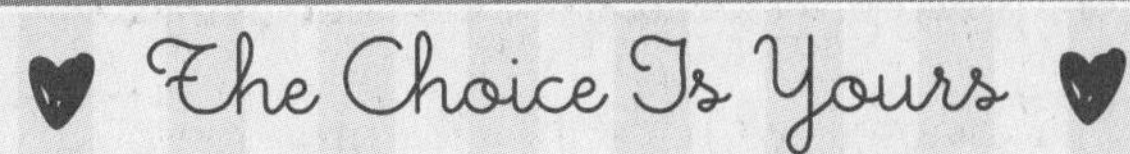

The Choice Is Yours

There is no question that choosing friends and making really good friendships is an important part of your life. Friends are one of the ways God encourages, teaches, trains, and grows you. It has been said that there are three kinds of people in life—

- those who pull you down,
- those who pull you along, and
- those who pull you up.

Be sure you choose friends who pull you up and along toward Jesus.

Oh, and don't forget to be the kind of friend who pulls others up and along toward Jesus!

Making Really Good Choices

In this chapter we have looked into God's Word and learned how important it is to choose the right kind of **F-R-I-E-N-D-S**. On this page, write out the point of each letter. (I'll get you started with "F.")

Finding a friend takes time.

R ______________________________

I ______________________________

E ______________________________

N ______________________________

D ______________________________

S ______________________________

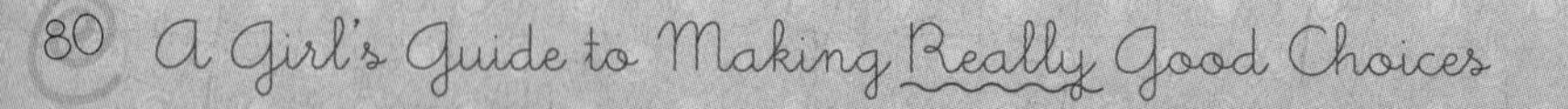

Now write out one thing you liked, learned, or want to do about finding good friends.

____

____

____

____

____

____

Take time now to seal your desire to make *really* good choices with the words of this prayer:

Dear Jesus, thank You for being my friend. I know You are always with me and will never leave me. Help me to encourage those around me, and guide me as I look for good friends who love You too. Amen.

6

Choosing What You Say... and Don't Say

"Go to your room right now, young lady," Megan's mother instructed as she pointed Megan toward her room.

Uh-oh! Megan knew she was in trouble—and she knew why. In fact, she knew it the very moment she opened her mouth to spew, "Heather, you're so stupid! Don't you know anything?"

Usually Megan was smarter and very skilled at putting down her sister when her mom wasn't around. She would make sure Mom was in another room or she and her sister were outside. But this time Megan had really messed up. Her mom had walked in while she was pouring out her latest dose of verbal abuse toward her sister, and had caught—or *heard*—Megan in the act!

Fun in God's Word!

Is your mouth ever important! Maybe right now yours is full of metal—which means your calendar is full of visits to your friendly orthodontist. And your mouth is also where you take in all the good food you need to grow up to be a girl after God's own heart.

And, of course, your mouth gives you the thrill of chewing gum and blowing enormous bubbles. And, unfortunately, many girls develop the bad habit of biting their fingernails—also done with the mouth.

Here are a few additional facts for you about the mouth:

What goes into your mouth is your choice.
What you do with your mouth is also your choice.
What comes *out* of your mouth—the words you say—is also your choice.

Your goal? As a girl who wants to make *really* good choices, your goal should be to choose that whatever comes out of your mouth is good. It's your choice.

You are not alone when it comes to saying things in anger or saying words that hurt someone. Believe me, I know how easy it is to get mad and lose it! It takes absolutely zero self-control and zero wisdom to spew out harsh words when you want to share exactly what you are thinking and feeling.

But God shows us a better way to use our mouths. He shows us His way. So once again, it's time to look at God's Word, the Bible, to find out what He says about your mouth. Got your pen in hand? Great! Now write down your answers as we look at some verses from the Bible. We are going to spell **M-O-U-T-H**.

Make your words pleasing to God. David, a man after God's own heart, was only a little older than you are when he wrote these words:

May these words of my mouth and this meditation of my heart be pleasing in your sight, LORD, my Rock and my Redeemer (Psalm 19:14).

What two things is God interested in according to this verse?

The ____

____

The ____

____

If you know what kinds of words please God, then you can choose what you will and will not use your mouth to say. Here are three verses that tell you what does *not* please God. As you read them, mark, circle, or underline everything God says you are to get rid of, especially when it comes to having a bad attitude:

Get rid of all bitterness, rage and anger, brawling and slander (Ephesians 4:31).

Nor should there be obscenity, foolish talk or coarse joking, which are out of place (Ephesians 5:4).

You must...rid yourselves of all such things as these: anger, rage, malice, slander, and filthy language from your lips. Do not lie to each other (Colossians 3:8-9).

Even when your emotions are running high, you still have a choice about what you say and don't say. It's possible you might choose to say things that hurt others or that harm the reputations of other people. Or you might choose to speak lies instead of the truth. But the right choice is to say words that bless and encourage others—which pleases God.

Look over the three passages above and your markings. Then list two of the things God hates—things that you will work on as you choose this week what you will and will not say:

1. ____

____

2. ____

____

Out of your heart your mouth speaks. This truth is right out of the Bible and was taught by Jesus. As a girl who follows God, I'm sure you want to be like Jesus. He always spoke the truth and used His mouth to teach about God and His will to those who gathered around Him. Here is one thing Jesus said about the mouth:

A good man brings good things out of the good stored up in his heart, and an evil man brings evil things out of the evil stored up in his heart. For the mouth speaks what the heart is full of (Luke 6:45).

Have you ever thought about the fact that what goes into your *heart* comes out of your *mouth*? The same is true of what you view with your eyes, what you read, even what you hear other people say or sing. If bad things are going into your head, heart, and mind, what, according to the verse above, will come out of your mouth?

____

____

____

I'm sure you got the right answer: When bad things go into your head, heart, and mind, bad things will come out of your mouth. That is what Jesus is saying. And the opposite is also true: What you view and read and hear that is good gets stored up in your heart. Then, because you have these good things in your heart, what does Jesus say will come out your mouth according to Luke 6:45?

____

____

____

Are you wondering what you should be storing up in your heart? What you should be thinking about? Do you want to know what will help good things to come out of your mouth? As you read this list of instructions, circle or underline the good things you are to think about. And here's a hint—there are eight of them.

Whatever is true, whatever is noble, whatever is right, whatever is pure, whatever is lovely, whatever is admirable—if anything is excellent or praiseworthy—think about such things (Philippians 4:8).

U**tter only what God says to say.** First, take a look at what God does *not* want you to say. Just as He is faithful to tell you what kinds of words and speech you *should* use your mouth for, He also tells you what you *should not* say.

Here are a few samples from Jesus' list. As you read along, don't forget to have your favorite pen or pencil ready. Mark these verses and circle key words. Underline what's important. Have fun in God's Word!

Anyone who says to a brother, "Raca," is answerable to the court (Matthew 5:22). (Just a note: The word "Raca" means "empty headed," or "dummy," or "stupid.")

Anyone who says, "You fool!" will be in danger of the fire of hell (also Matthew 5:22).

Name-calling is not acceptable to God. Look again at the verse above. Then list here two things Jesus never wants to hear you say to anyone:

1. ____

____

2. ____

____

Do not let any unwholesome talk come out of your mouths, but only what is helpful for building others up according to their needs, that it may benefit those who listen (Ephesians 4:29).

What kind of talk does God say should never come out of your mouth?

____

____

Instead, what kinds of words should you speak?

Words that ______________________ others.

Words that __________________ others up.

Truth is always the right thing to say. How would you feel if your parents or a good friend lied to you, and did not tell you the truth? That would hurt, wouldn't it? Would you find it hard to trust anything else your parents or friend said to you?

Lying hurts people. It damages family relationships and friendships. When you lie, it means you have something to hide, or something you don't want other people to know about or find out. That's why telling a lie is like building a brick wall between you and the person you lie to. Lies are like walls that push people further apart.

Can you see why lying is so harmful? That is why the Bible commands us not to lie:

> *Therefore, putting away lying, "Let each one of you speak truth with his neighbor"* (Ephesians 4:25 NKJV).

What does God want you to do about lying?

____

____

What does God want you to do instead of lying?

____

____

____

Here is more advice from God: *Do not lie to each other* (Colossians 3:9).

It is obvious, but go ahead and write out God's command to you in Colossians 3:9:

____

____

Hurting someone with your words is wrong. Do you have a fireplace where you live? Or have you been camping and built a campfire for roasting marshmallows for s'mores? Or have you ever watched a TV news channel when it showed a wildfire out of control? There is no doubt that any kind of fire can do a lot of damage to many people. Physical fire can be very destructive.

Did you know that the Bible says your mouth and the hurtful words you speak are as destructive as a raging fire? Here's what it says:

> *The tongue also is a fire, a world of evil among the parts of the body. It corrupts the whole body, sets the whole course of one's life on fire, and is itself set on fire by hell* (James 3:6).

Fill in the blanks to see how serious the effects of your tongue and words can be:

The tongue is like a __________________

It's a world of ______________________________

It ________________________ the whole person

It sets the whole person's life on ___________

Here's another helpful truth, once again out of Ephesians 4:29: *Do not let any unwholesome talk come out of your mouths, but only what is helpful for building others up.*

What word is used to describe the hurtful and bad words that come out of your mouth?

____

Just a note: "Unwholesome" is another word for foul, rotten, corrupt, icky, gross, or spoiled.

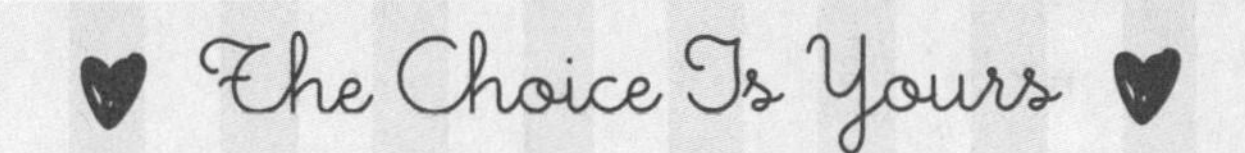

The Choice Is Yours

I'm sure you already know that once you say something bad to someone, you cannot take it back. You said it. They heard you say it. And even if you say you are sorry, you have hurt another person, and still have to admit that what you said came out of *your* very own heart! When you say something bad, it is a sign something is wrong in your heart.

Like all the other choices you make, making *really* good choices starts with your heart. So make sure you put God's Word into your heart. Then what comes out from your mouth will be God's thoughts and God's words—which are always 100 percent good.

And here's another important point: One really good choice you can make is the choice to think carefully before you speak. In other words, control your mouth. Make this the prayer of your heart. It will help!

> *Set a guard over my mouth, Lord;*
> *keep watch over the door of my lips* (Psalm 141:3).

If you control your mouth and what you say, the Bible says you will be *perfect, able to keep* [your] *whole body in check* (James 3:2). What a great goal to work toward! And, once again, the choice is yours. You can choose to say mean things to people—or not. You can choose to call them names and make them feel bad, or you can choose to speak kind words, words of love and friendship.

The choice is yours. God wants you to speak in ways that are good. Will you take God seriously about this, or not? If you choose to say what He says is right, and choose to not say what He says is wrong, you will truly be a girl after God's own heart.

Making Really Good Choices

In this chapter we have looked into God's Word and learned about godly speech. On this page write out the point of each letter below. (I'll get you started with "M.")

Make your words pleasing to God.

O ______________________________

U ______________________________

T ______________________________

H ______________________________

Now write out one thing you liked, learned, or want to do about what comes out of your mouth—and what doesn't!

Take time now to seal your desire to make *really* good choices with the words of this prayer:

Dear Jesus, help me to stop, wait, and remember Your guidelines about my words before I say anything. I really need Your help in choosing to speak only what honors You and does good to others. Amen.

7

Choosing to Be Patient

"Be patient, Megan, please! You are just about to drive me crazy!" Megan's mom was beginning to get a little impatient herself with Megan's selfish, demanding behavior. Once again, trying to make Megan understand, her mother said, "We'll get to your craft project just as soon as I finish calling people to take meals to the Barnes family. Mrs. Barnes needs some help for the next few days now that she had her baby."

Megan was beside herself. It seemed like everything and everyone was standing in the way of her getting what she wanted. She could understand why taking her little sister to the doctor with a high fever was an okay reason why her mom hadn't ordered the supplies for her project. But that new baby in someone else's home was just about more than Megan could take!

Couldn't her mom see how much this project meant to her? She had tried and tried to convince her mother, but her mom seemed to have many other more important things to do. Megan was so upset that she stomped down the hall to her favorite place—her room—slammed the door, and flopped on her bed.

"Be patient!" she hissed. "I think I have been very patient. I think it's about time for my mom to start thinking about me for a change, and about what I want!"

Fun in God's Word!

It's obvious that Megan had made a choice. Rather than see how she could be a help to her mom with some really important concerns, like the needs of others, she chose to storm out of the room. She didn't realize that God wanted her to be patient. She didn't understand that patience was God's gift to Megan so she could be a blessing to her mom and others rather than a pain.

It's time again to look at God's Word and find out how He wants you, His girl, to act when you are asked to wait. So you know what to do, right? Grab your pen and write down your answers as we look at some verses from the Bible. We are going to spell out **P-A-T-I-E-N-C-E**.

Patience is learning to wait. We might say that patience is learning to do nothing! I know you probably enjoy "doing nothing" and having days when you get to be lazy. But this is different. This is doing nothing when it is the right choice to make. Patience is...

Doing nothing when you are told to wait after school.
Doing nothing when kids make fun of you at school.

Doing nothing instead of getting mad and angry.
Doing nothing instead of getting even.

Here's how Jesus explained patience to His disciple, Peter:

Then Peter came to Jesus and asked, "Lord, how many times shall I forgive my brother or sister who sins against me? Up to seven times?" (Matthew 18:21).

What did Peter think was the maximum number of times he should forgive someone?

________________________________ times

Jesus said to him, "I do not say to you, up to seven times, but up to seventy times seven" (Matthew 18:22 NASB).

You do the math! According to Jesus, patience does not stop with forgiving someone seven times. No, He said *seventy times seven*. How many times is 70 x 7?

____

The point Jesus was making is this: You should always be willing to forgive. Can you imagine how much patience that is going to require on your part?

Ask God for patience. Learning to wait is not easy. That is where prayer comes to your rescue. God is willing to give you *His* patience whenever you ask for it. So ask! Then you can follow through on this command from God:

Be patient, bearing with one another in love (Ephesians 4:2).

List two things you can do to be more patient the next time you have to wait or don't get what you want or someone upsets you:

____

____

____

While you are thinking about patience, think about Noah. You probably know the story of Noah and the ark. God told Noah to build an ark so Noah could gather up two of every living creature and survive a flood that would destroy the world and the people in it because they were evil. Here's what the Bible reports:

God waited patiently in the days of Noah while the ark was being built (1 Peter 3:20).

Genesis 6:3 tells us that God waited and gave the wicked people of the world *a hundred and twenty years* to turn away from their sin!

So, how long did God wait patiently?

____

Hopefully this encourages you to be more patient!

Take ten. You have probably heard this saying: "Count to ten before you say anything." Or "Count to ten before you do anything." This little bit of advice trains you to wait—to patiently do nothing until you can say or do the right thing. It keeps you from losing your temper or hurting someone physically or with your words.

The apostle Paul faced his share of insults and people lying about him. But he was patient. What advice does he give about how you should respond to people who say things that hurt you?

> *The Lord's bond-servant must not be quarrelsome*...[but] *patient when wronged* (2 Timothy 2:24 NASB).

When I am wronged I am *not* to...

____

Instead I am to...

____

Ignore insults. Don't you just hate it when someone calls you a name or makes fun of you? What is usually your first reaction? If you are like most people, you want to give an insult right back, don't you? She called you a name, so you immediately want to call her a name!

Well, patience also applies to the insults you receive. Here's a verse that teaches us about patience:

A person's wisdom yields [produces] *patience; it is to one's glory to overlook an offense* (Proverbs 19:11).

According to this verse, what kind of person has or grows in patience?

____

____

To be patient is a mark of wisdom—only a wise person has patience. So remember what you have been learning: Be wise and count to ten.

What does this same verse tell you to do when someone insults you?

____

____

____

God's message is be wise, be patient, and be forgiving. Make patience your first reaction when others are rude or make fun of you.

Endurance is a part of waiting. Soooo, how long can you wait? You might say, "Well, that depends. I could wait forever before I get punished for getting mad at my little sister. But I can't wait very long at all when I want to work on my new craft project."

Always remember that the willingness to wait is not based on what you *think* is right, but on what *is* right. That's a lesson King Saul in the Old Testament failed to learn. God's prophet Samuel told King Saul:

Go down ahead of me to Gilgal. I will surely come down to you to sacrifice burnt offerings...but you must wait seven days until I come to you and tell you what you are to do (1 Samuel 10:8).

What was King Saul told to do, and for how long?

____

____

____

What was Samuel going to do when he arrived in seven days?

____

____

____

The story continues: *He* [Saul] *waited seven days, the time set by Samuel; but Samuel did not come to Gilgal, and Saul's men began to scatter. So he said, "Bring me the burnt offering..." And Saul offered up the burnt offering* (1 Samuel 13:8-9).

What happened when the prophet Samuel did not arrive on the seventh day?

____

____

Then, sure enough, Samuel showed up on the scene. When Samuel saw what Saul had done, he said, *You have done a foolish thing* (1 Samuel 13:13). How did Samuel describe Saul's lack of patience?

____

____

Because Saul was in a hurry and did not wait patiently for Samuel, he went ahead and offered up the animal sacrifices himself. So Samuel said to King Saul:

You have not kept the command the LORD *your God gave you; if you had, he would have established your kingdom over Israel for all time. But now your kingdom will not endure* (1 Samuel 13:13-14).

Underline the result or consequence of King Saul's disobedience to God's prophet and his failure to wait as instructed.

N**ever try to get even.** You already know how easy it is to want to hurt someone back because they hurt you. You want to get even, right? But God shows you a better way—His way.

Do not repay evil with evil or insult with insult. On the contrary, repay evil with blessing (1 Peter 3:9).

What are you *not* to do in response to evil or insults?

____

____

What are you to do instead?

____

____

(Just a note: Here, "blessing" means to speak well of that person.)

Carry Jesus' example in your heart. Few people have ever experienced as much pain and abuse as Jesus did. It is very hard not to get angry and upset when someone picks on you and hurts you physically. But Jesus, who is the perfect example of patience, suffered far more hurt than we ever will. How did He respond to His enemies? This next verse tells us these details about His patience toward those who were cruel to Him:

When they hurled their insults at him, he [Jesus] *did not retaliate; when he suffered, he made no threats. Instead, he entrusted himself to him* [God] *who judges justly* (1 Peter 2:23).

Underline how Jesus showed patience by what He did *not* do.

What did Jesus do instead?

____

____

____

After the soldiers nailed Jesus to a cross, He prayed:

"Father, forgive them, for they do not know what they are doing" (Luke 23:34).

What was the message or the heart of Jesus' prayer?

____

____

Is there anyone you need to forgive who has hurt you in some way? Pray for them now!

Even out your temper. Do you know what a *hothead* is? It's a person who does not control his or her temper. It is also a terrible weakness. Read on to learn what the Bible says about people who *can* control their temper. Look at this verse, then fill in the blanks below:

He who is slow to anger is better than the mighty [a warrior], *and he who rules his spirit than he who takes* [or conquers] *a city* (Proverbs 16:32 NKJV).

A person who is even-tempered and slow to anger is better than

____

____

A person who can rule his or her spirit or temper is more valued than a soldier or even an army who can ___________________________ a city.

It takes a lot of strength to be patient. The easy thing to do is blow up and lose control. But to do the opposite—to choose to be patient—is a sign of great power and self-control.

Here's something to think about: How strong are you when it comes to ruling your spirit?

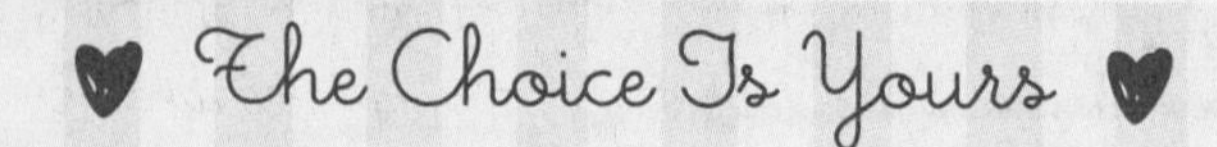

There is no doubt that it is a real challenge to be patient. That's why this topic is included in this book—it's *very* important! You will always have opportunities to be patient when others are mean, or say mean things, or make you wait for something. So how can you grow to be more and more patient?

Here's an idea that comes straight from the Bible—*clothe [yourself] with...patience* (Colossians 3:12). Just like you go to your closet every day and choose what you are going to wear, you need to go to God's closet and choose to put on patience—*His* patience.

My friend, the choice is yours. You get to choose whether you will or will not obey God's commands to be patient—whether you will or will not *work* on being patient. So make your first choice to put on patience and clothe yourself with it. Try it for a day. *Everyone* will be glad you did! Especially God.

Making Really Good Choices

In this chapter we have looked into God's Word and learned how important it is to have **P-A-T-I-E-N-C-E**. On this page, write out the point of each letter. (I'll get you started with "P.")

Now write out one thing you liked, learned, or want to do about choosing to wait, or having patience.

____

____

____

____

____

____

Take time now to seal your desire to make *really* good choices with the words of this prayer:

Lord, You know what a hard time I have waiting. And now I know what I have to do: I must learn to wait! I can hardly wait until I get dressed tomorrow to "put on" some patience. I really need it around my house...and at school...and...and... and! Thank You for Your help—and Your example. Amen.

8

Choosing a Happy Heart

"Megan," Dad's deep voice interrupted as she sat at the breakfast table stuffing her mouth full of waffles, "don't forget. Tomorrow I need you and your sister to help me and Mom do some work around here to get ready for our annual Christmas open house."

"Well, that certainly wasn't very good news," Megan growled as she escaped to her room after breakfast. No way was Megan happy about what Dad had just dropped on her. She already had big plans for her Saturday, and they sure didn't include helping her parents get ready for a party for a bunch of grown-ups!

Suddenly the joy Megan was experiencing a few minutes ago when she was enjoying her day—and her waffles!—turned black. She wanted her family—and the whole world—to know how displeased she was, so she closed the door to her room harder—and louder—than usual.

The next morning, Megan heard a knock on her bed-room door. She opened her eyes to the sound of her mom telling her to, of all things, "Rise and shine! Breakfast is on the table. Then we've got a lot of work to do to get ready for the party."

Do you know what a crossroad is? I'm sure you have been with your parents in the car when you were on a vacation and came to a place where several roads met. That's a crossroad.

Maybe the scene played out something like this: Your dad was convinced he needed to continue to go straight. Mom, however, who had the GPS device and a map in her lap, said he needed to turn left. In other words, there were different ways they could go. That's how it is with many decisions we make. We find ourselves at a crossroad, and a choice needs to be made.

Well, our young friend Megan is also at a crossroad. Oh, she isn't driving a car! After all, she's only 11. No, her crossroad is whether she is going to choose to be happy or sad and grumpy. Ever since her dad had given her the "good" news about his and Mom's plans for her Saturday, she had been anything but happy. How about mad?

Yes, Megan was at a crossroad with her attitude. She could go one way and choose to have a happy heart and pitch in wholeheartedly and be helpful to her family. Or she could choose another direction and come out of her room with a bad attitude. With this choice she could probably ruin the day for everyone. A choice to be grumpy and sullen would cause her to be more of a hindrance to the family project than a helper.

What choice will Megan make?

Fun in God's Word!

Has your mom or dad ever told you to go to your room and not come out until you have a "happy heart"? If so, you were probably acting like Megan did after hearing about the Saturday work plans. You were upset that things weren't going your way. So you chose to be grumpy.

Well, do you want to know what it really means to have a happy heart? Then it is time to look at God's Word, the Bible, again. Let's find out how God wants you, His girl, to act when you are disappointed, when you aren't getting what you want. How are you going to respond to something you don't want or like to do, but are being told you must do it anyway?

It's pen and pencil time. Get ready to write down some answers as we look at verses from the Bible. We are going to really enjoy spelling out **J-O-Y**.

Jesus shows you how to have joy. There is a difference between happiness and joy, between being happy and being joyful. To begin with, happiness is a feeling. Being happy comes because something pleasant is happening in your life. When you get what you want, you are happy. And when you get to do what you want, you are happy. And, like Megan, when you don't get what you want, or you don't get to do what you want to do, then you are unhappy.

Jesus is the perfect example of a person who didn't have a lot of good things happen to Him. Here are two verses that describe some of the difficult things that Jesus experienced. After each verse write out the problem Jesus faced.

Jesus replied, "Foxes have dens and birds have nests, but the Son of Man [Jesus] *has no place to lay his head"* (Matthew 8:20).

____

____

____

For forty days he [Jesus] *was tempted by the devil. He ate nothing during those days, and at the end of them he was hungry* (Luke 4:2).

____

____

____

You can see from just these few examples how Jesus was often hungry, and He had no home. In addition, He suffered physical pain, and people laughed at Him, mocked Him, and made fun of Him. Now read the next scripture. What does it say you should do when things are not going your way?

Fixing our eyes on Jesus, the pioneer and perfecter of faith... (Hebrews 12:2)

____

____

____

Take a look at the rest of this verse and write the word that is used to describe Jesus' attitude as He faced difficulties and trouble. (And don't forget to notice that the word *happy* is not used!)

> *For the joy set before him* [Jesus] *endured the cross, scorning its shame* (Hebrews 12:2).

____

What are some of the things that cause you to be happy? Getting your allowance? Reading your new book? Finish this sentence with some of your favorite things: I am the most happy when...

____

____

____

As you already know, life is not always filled with fun and games and good things. So what is it that upsets you? Your parents telling you *no* when you want to go somewhere with your friends? *No* when you want to watch TV or play on the computer? List some of the things that upset you or make you mad—things that can ruin your day.

____

____

____

As you have been learning, you can be joyful no matter what is going on in your life. You are *not* always around happy and pleasant people. And things do *not* always go your way. But you can still be joyful because your joy comes from following Jesus' example. When you live like Jesus, you will show joy at all times, even when things are not the way you want them to be.

When your parents want you to have a "happy heart," what they are really asking is that you have a "joyful heart." A joyful heart is a heart that experiences joy no matter what is happening around you, even if it is unpleasant.

Take a minute to think about Megan. Like all parents, yours ask you to do things you don't want to do—like putting the trash can out...and bringing it back in. Or like watching over your little sister while she is outside playing. Or taking your turn at clearing the dirty dishes off the table. How do you usually respond when you don't want to do what you are asked? What do you say, and how do you act?

____

____

____

____

Think of a new and better way to respond with joy the next time you are asked to do something. Or, put another way, what choices will you make about your words, attitude, and actions?

Next time, I want to

____

____

____

Observe others who are joyful. Are you wondering how being joyful is better than being happy? Good question! Well, it helps to remember that being happy depends on how *good* things are in your day and your life. But you can have joy no matter how *bad* things get around you. Use your pen to write down how the people in the following examples responded to their troubles.

Scene 1: In the Bible, we read that Peter and John were whipped by the Jewish religious leaders because they preached about Jesus. Write out how these two men responded to their beating, and why.

After their beating *the apostles left the Sanhedrin, rejoicing because they had been counted worthy of suffering disgrace for the Name* [of Jesus] (Acts 5:41).

____

____

____

Scene 2: The apostle Paul and his friend Silas were put in jail for preaching about Jesus. Write out their response to being chained up, and the response of their fellow prisoners.

About midnight Paul and Silas were praying and singing hymns to God, and the other prisoners were listening to them (Acts 16:25).

Paul and Silas ________________________________

____

The other prisoners ____________________________

____

It is always good to notice the positive examples of others who suffered and their response to difficulties or trials. How does the Bible say *you* are to respond to things that are not what you would like them to be?

Consider it pure joy, my brothers and sisters, whenever you face trials of many kinds (James 1:2).

____

____

____

Saturdays are super special, aren't they? I mean, usually there is no schoolwork, no alarm clock, no getting up early. This isn't always true, but every girl looks forward to

Saturdays when she can kick back, hang out, and have some fun. You worked hard all week, and you deserve a break, right?

But what if your parents ask you to do some work, or to go with them to visit your grandpa in the hospital, or to help dad rake leaves, or a bunch of other things you think are going to be boring, and you are required to do them anyway? Think back—and maybe even take a look back at the examples in this section—and answer this question: How did Jesus, Peter and John, and Paul and Silas respond to unpleasant things?

____

____

Your parents and teachers and others in authority will always be asking you to do things you don't want to do. According to what you have been learning, how should you respond?

____

____

____

____

____

Yield to God. To *yield* means to give in or give power to another person. When you yield to God—and not to sin—you will experience joy. You will have peace of mind. And you will not have to experience the painful consequences that come from making bad choices!

Your goal should be to follow God no matter what. That means you obey Him and do things His way. How can you yield to God and obey Him, according to this verse?

How can a young person stay on the path of purity? By living according to your word [the Bible] (Psalm 119:9).

____

____

____

The next verse says, *I seek you with all my heart; do not let me stray from your commands* (Psalm 119:10).

How strongly should you want to obey God?

____

____

____

What should your prayer be?

The next verse is filled with good advice: *I have hidden your word* [Bible verses] *in my heart that I might not sin against you* (Psalm 119:11). When you memorize Bible verses, how do they help you to obey God?

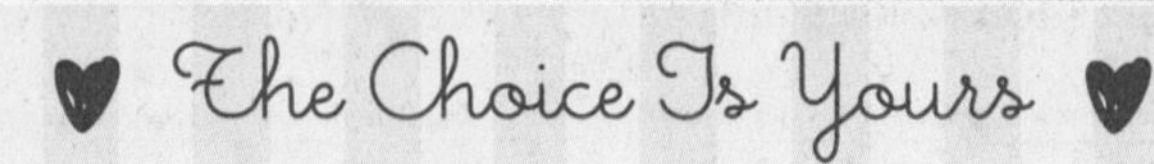

The Choice Is Yours

How exciting it is to know that reading your Bible and following the examples of Jesus and other godly people will help you have joy. You can choose to be joyful and have a happy heart every time you pitch in and help the family and do it with a good attitude. Sure, it may not be the way you want to spend your time, but it is what God is asking you to do. And you can grit your teeth, sneer, sigh, grumble, and do it—or you can make a *really* good choice and do it *with all your heart, as working for the Lord, not for human masters* (Colossians 3:23).

Now, let's revisit Megan's situation—only it is *you!* It's Saturday, which Dad has declared a "work day." You have a *really* big choice to make: How are you going to act when you come out of your room for breakfast? What kind of heart will you choose to have as you walk toward the breakfast table and join the family? Based on what you have been learning about joy and a happy heart, what choice will you (hopefully!) make?

____

____

____

____

Making Really Good Choices

In this chapter we have looked into God's Word and learned how important it is to make **J-O-Y** a habit. On this page, write out the point of each letter. (I'll get you started with "J.")

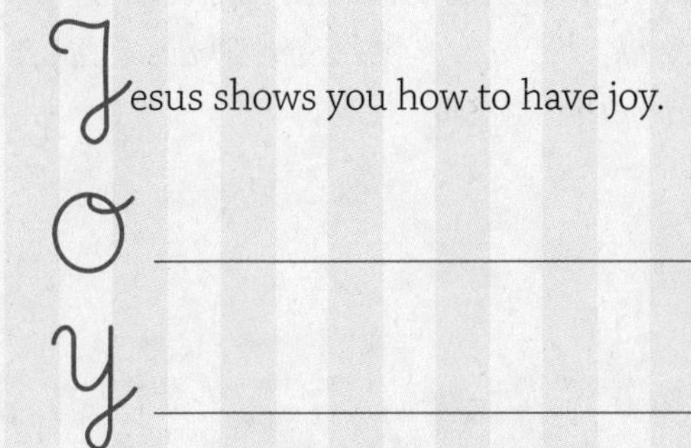

Now write out one thing you liked, learned, or want to do about choosing to have a happy heart.

____

____

____

____

____

____

Take time now to seal your desire to make *really* good choices with the words of this prayer:

> *Dear Jesus, help me understand that real joy is found in You, and in being like You. I ask that You give me Your joy even when things aren't going my way. And just between You and me, Lord, I really like the way I feel when I have a happy heart. I need more of that. Amen.*

9

Choosing to Be Faithful

Megan's day turned out pretty well, even though things didn't start out so great. Too bad she was late to school and didn't get any time with her best friend, Brittany, before school started. Her only other problem came in English class when she tried to explain to her teacher why she hadn't finished her English paper. But now school was over, along with all the school issues. It was all behind her as she sailed into the rest of her day. Megan was so looking forward to reading more of her new book when she got back home. "Ah, I can't wait to get home," she sighed.

Megan's feet had barely touched the living room floor when her mother pounced on her. Her mom had that look that told Megan she was in *b-i-g* trouble. Sternly she asked, "Megan, did you forget something this morning before you ran out of the house for school? Did you forget to feed Fluffy?" (Megan hated it when her mom asked a question they both knew the answer to.)

"Well, Mom," Megan began her defense, "you know I was running behind this morning, and I didn't want to be late for school." (Gulp! Megan couldn't help but remember some of the bad choices she had made that morning—well, and the night before!—that caused her to be late for school.)

Megan's weak answer gave Mom the perfect opportunity to remind Megan of a promise she had made. "Megan, you begged your dad and me for a puppy. Remember? And you promised that if we would get you a puppy, you would take care of it and feed it every morning and take it out before school. Remember? Well, you promised, and now you've got Fluffy, but you are not living up to your promise—like this morning. You are failing to keep your word and take care of Fluffy."

Fun in God's Word!

This is only the latest episode in which Megan has not come through on her promises. Just ask her Bible competition teammates at church, or the girls on her soccer team about how she chose to skip practice because she was "just too tired." Tales of Megan letting people down go on and on, but I'm sure you get the picture. It is obvious that Megan doesn't understand how important it is to be faithful. She must not know that being faithful means being loyal, trustworthy, and dependable.

And maybe she doesn't know that the Bible also has a *l-o-t* to say about faithfulness. Faithfulness is an important choice that Megan—and you too as a girl who wants to please God and your parents—needs to understand and practice.

So now it's time once again to look to the Bible, and find out what God says about being faithful. With pen in hand, write down your answers as we look up some verses from the Bible. We are going to spell **F-A-I-T-H-F-U-L**.

Faithfulness is a fruit of the Spirit. If you are a Christian, God's Holy Spirit is living in you. His role is to help you do what pleases God. Below, circle the specific "fruit" we are talking about in this chapter.

> *The fruit of the Spirit is love, joy, peace, forbearance, kindness, goodness, faithfulness, gentleness and self-control* (Galatians 5:22-23).

> Just a note: In the Bible, the word "faithful" basically means "loyal, constant, reliable, sure," and "true." It's a tall order from God, and His Spirit is always available to help you be faithful.

> As you begin this chapter about faithfulness, how would you rate your faithfulness last week at home, in your schoolwork, and your other commitments? Circle one.

Very faithful   Sort of faithful   Needs improvement

Act like God and be faithful. From the beginning of the Bible to the last page, you can see that God is faithful. Let's start with one of the first books of the Bible. While praising God, what did Moses say about God?

He is the Rock, his works are perfect, and all his ways are just. A faithful God who does no wrong... (Deuteronomy 32:4).

God is ______________________________

God is ______________________________

God is ______________________________

God is ______________________________

In the middle of the Bible, we read the words of a man who is praising God. What did he want the world to know about God?

With my mouth I will make your faithfulness known through all generations (Psalm 89:1).

____

____

In the last book in the Bible, what is Jesus, God's Son, called when He returns to earth?

I saw heaven standing open and there before me was a white horse, whose rider is called Faithful and True (Revelation 19:11).

____

____

As a girl who wants to follow God, faithfulness like His should be part of your character. That is why it is important to choose to be faithful in everything you do, whether it's feeding the dog, memorizing Scripture verses to support your Bible club teammates, doing your homework every evening, or getting up in the morning, doing your chores, and getting to school on time.

Insights into faithfulness. Do you know what *insight* means? It means to gain a better understanding of something. When it comes to being faithful, we can say that a girl who shows this quality in her life is reliable. People can count on her, especially her parents. And we can say that God can count on her too. People can trust her in what she says and what she does.

Here are a few traits that describe a faithful girl. Check the ones you need to work on more, with God's help.

_____She follows through on whatever she has to do.

_____She finishes what she starts, no matter what.

_____She shows up early so others won't worry.

_____She keeps her word. If she makes a promise, she keeps it.

_____She attends church regularly and does her Sunday school lesson.

Choose and write down the mark of faithfulness that you will start working on today.

____

____

____

The marks of faithfulness. Right about now, you may be wondering, "How can I produce this fruit of *faithfulness*?" As always, God has the answer. In the verse below, how does Jesus say you can start proving your faithfulness and begin to strengthen this character quality each day?

He who is faithful in a very little thing is faithful also in much (Luke 16:10 NASB).

____

____

____

Deciding to be faithful in the small things is a *really* good choice. What is a good habit to develop that will help you fulfill your responsibilities, starting at home?

[She] *does not eat the bread of idleness* (Proverbs 31:27).

____

____

____

The Bible describes an important quality for church leaders as well as for all of God's people, including you. What does this verse say that quality is?

Deacons...[and] *their wives must be...faithful in all things* (1 Timothy 3:10-11 NKJV).

____

____

____

Now go back and circle the word "all."

Heroes because of faithfulness. Are you looking for an example of a young person who was faithful? In the Bible, we find a great example in the young teenage boy named Daniel. He and three of his friends were taken captive from Israel and moved far away to Babylon. There, the king of Babylon offered them food that God's law did not allow them to eat.

Think about it: Daniel and his friends were in a foreign land, separated from their parents. There was no one around to tell them what to do. They were free to do whatever they wanted. How did Daniel and his friends show their faithfulness to God?

Daniel resolved not to defile himself with the royal food and wine (Daniel 1:8).

____

____

____

Now go back and circle the word "not."

How else did Daniel's three friends show their faithfulness to God when they were commanded to worship a golden image or be punished and put to death?

We want you to know, Your Majesty, that we will not serve your gods or worship the image of gold you have set up (Daniel 3:18).

____

____

____

Once again, circle the word "not."

Faithfulness is always a right choice. You will never be successful in anything you wish to do well without being faithful in the little things as well as the big things. Whatever you want to do now, tomorrow, next week, or next year will only be accomplished with faithfulness. Faithfulness is needed every step of the way...and throughout every day. For instance:

Your homework—Going to school, learning, and growing in knowledge will require work on your part, which includes doing homework. Your teachers will not give you more work than you can do, and there are reasons they give you assignments. What does this verse say about why you are to do your best in everything, which includes your schoolwork?

And whatever you do, whether in word or deed, do it all in the name of the Lord Jesus (Colossians 3:17).

___

___

___

Your devotions—This subject is not a surprise, is it? Having devotions—spending some time reading your Bible and praying—is a choice you must faithfully make each day. It is a choice that will help guide you to make *really* good choices all day long. How will that be achieved? By faithfully reading God's Word every day. What did King David desire to do each day?

You, God, are my God, earnestly I seek you (Psalm 63:1).

___

___

Just a note: The rest of this verse goes on to say, *I thirst for you, my whole being longs for you, in a dry and parched land where there is no water.* As soon as David woke up, he was thirsty for God. He wanted—and needed—to spend time with God.

Your friends—You need to be a faithful friend. Part of this includes being faithful to choose the right kind of friends—that is, friends who love Jesus. Then be faithful to them. Stand with them, as Daniel stood with his friends against their enemies. Stick together against the challenges you all face at school.

U**nreliable is the opposite of faithful.** We can learn a lot from opposites. And the opposite of faithful is *unreliable*. An unreliable person fails to come through on their commitments, cannot be depended on, and cannot be trusted with information or responsibility.

John Mark is a sad case of a young man who was not faithful. The apostle Paul went on an important missionary trip and he took John Mark with him to be on his team as a helper. His story is told in Acts 12:25–13:13. For now, describe what happened when things got difficult in one area of their ministry and the team had to sail to another location.

From Paphos, Paul and his companions sailed to Perga in Pamphylia, where John left them to return to Jerusalem (Acts 13:13).

____

____

Here's something to think about:

You can depend on the Lord,
but can He depend on you?

Laziness is the opposite of faithfulness. Laziness is the most natural thing you can do. It's so easy to do nothing! That's why faithfulness is such a challenge. It requires God's help to power up and do what you have to do and need to do, no matter what.

The hard thing about being faithful is that you live with a constant temptation to do nothing...or to do as little as possible. Laziness says, "I don't want to do it." Laziness whines, "I don't want to do my chores...I don't want to get up and check on my little brother...I don't want to feed the dog...I don't want to read my Bible."

Are you wondering where you can get the strength you need to be faithful? Praise God you can choose to go to Him whenever you need to be faithful, even when you would rather be lazy and do nothing. Read these two verses that will help you when you need to be faithful:

The LORD is the stronghold of my life (Psalm 27:1).

I can do all this through him [Jesus] *who gives me strength* (Philippians 4:13).

How does God help you with the strength to be faithful...

in Psalm 27:1?

in Philippians 4:13?

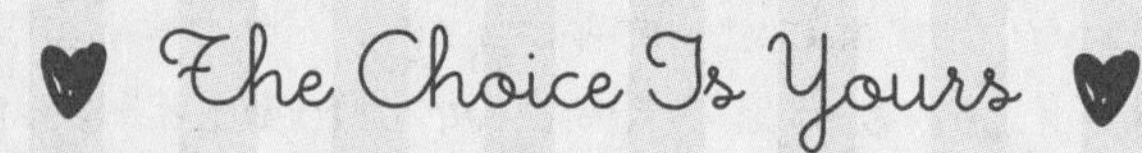

The Choice Is Yours

Faithfulness is such a rare quality. Do you realize that if you walk in faithfulness, you will become a hero—like Daniel and his young friends? They chose to do the right thing and be faithful when it wasn't easy for them to do so.

What does the word *hero* mean to you? How do you think God is calling you to be a hero at your home or in your school?

Making Really Good Choices

In this chapter we have looked into God's Word and learned how to be **F-A-I-T-H-F-U-L**. On this page write out the point of each letter. (I'll get you started with "F.")

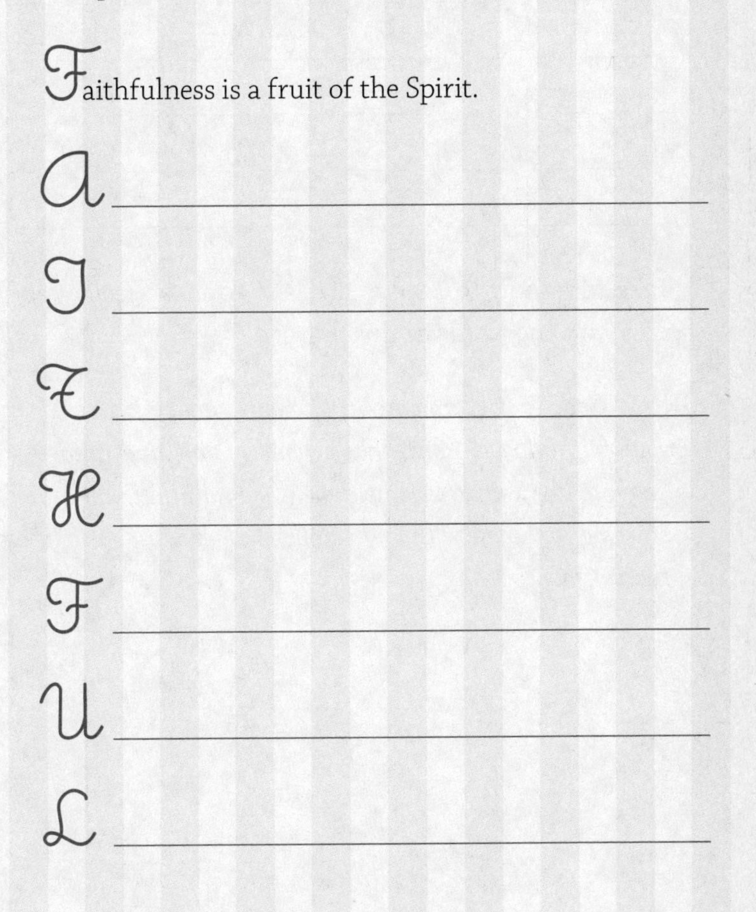

Now write out one thing you liked, learned, or want to do about being faithful.

____

____

____

____

____

____

Take time now to seal your desire to make *really* good choices with the words of this prayer:

Dear God, Your Word says in Lamentations 3:23, "Great is your faithfulness." Lord, that's what I want and need—to be more like You. Please help me to be faithful in all things, starting at home with my family and my responsibilities there. Amen.

10

Choosing to Trust God

Megan had made some really bad choices this past week. And it all started with choosing not to get up. It seemed like such a *tiny* thing! But looking back, Megan could see how that choice started a downhill slide in her week.

With that first less-than-stellar choice came the second one—to not have her devotions and prayer time. After all, when you get up late, there's no way to fit in a quiet time!

Well, those choices were personal. But then she chose to be unkind to others, to be grumpy to her family, and to not help out at home.

And in her heart? She knew what she was doing when she chose the "in crowd" over her church friends, and even snubbed her best friend in hopes of becoming one of the popular girls at school.

Yes, Megan felt like a total failure. It had been a really bad week. No, to be more accurate, it had been a lot of bad weeks in a row! In fact, Megan had a hard time remembering the last time she had made a good or right choice on her own. Usually, when things got too bad, her parents stepped in and made sure she went to bed on time, she got up on time, and she wore the right kinds of clothes to school. On and on her parents-to-the-rescue list went.

Deep inside Megan knew she was old enough to make most of these decisions on her own. But she was choosing—yes, *choosing*—to be lazy, stubborn, and to go against what she knew she needed to do. She also knew it was because she just honestly did not *want* to make good choices...which led to her parents having to force her to do the right things.

And now it's Sunday. Maybe because it's time to go to church, Megan is realizing how bad she feels about her failure to do the things that would please her parents, and most of all, please God. With a sense of utter defeat and confusion, she slowly slides into a seat in her girls' class at church. For once, her sorrow is real and heartfelt.

About this time Miss Julie, her Sunday school teacher, began her talk to the girls from Proverbs 3:5-6.

Fun in God's Word!

Megan had always been on the fringe of her Christian friends and their circle. It was her choice, of course. Sure, she always went to church. (Her parents made sure of that!) And she was attending the Sunday school class for preteen girls. But she had never really tuned in to what was happening there (again, her choice).

Instead, Megan chose to live with one foot in the world and one foot in the Christian scene. At times she would act the way her parents told her to act. On the outside, she would obey, but on the inside she was rebelling by being mean to her little sister, giving her parents a hard time, and being a problem for her teachers at school. She didn't like being a mean girl.

Yes, Megan knew in her soul that she was at another crossroad. On this memorable Sunday, she was having some big struggles. She knew in her heart that she had made a lot of bad choices, especially about the way she was acting.

As Megan sat in her class with her head down, she knew she had to make a firm choice to stop being influenced by the world and start living for Jesus. Maybe, just maybe, something Miss Julie would say might help! For the first time in a *l-o-n-g* time, she made an effort to listen—to really, *really* listen.

Now, let's pretend we are sitting next to Megan in her Sunday school class. And let's listen as Miss Julie begins taking the girls through a passage in the Bible. Miss Julie is about to walk her girls (and you!) through a study about trusting God. So once again, grab your pen and write down your answers as we look at some verses from the Bible. We are going to spell **T-R-U-S-T**.

Miss Julie begins the class by saying, "Open your Bibles." (Yay! For the first time in a long while, Megan had remembered to bring her Bible to church.) Miss Julie added, "Turn with me to the book of Proverbs, chapter 3, and let's take a look at verses 5 and 6." Then Miss Julie read the verses out loud:

Trust in the LORD with all your heart and do not lean on your own understanding. In all your ways acknowledge Him, and He will make your paths straight (NASB).

Trust in the Lord. *Trust in the LORD with all your heart* (verse 5)—Do you ever feel like there's no one you can trust, or no one who understands what you are going through when you have an important decision to make? It's awful feeling so alone! Sometimes your parents don't relate to your problem. And your friends are little or no help. You feel like there is a heavy weight on your young shoulders. So you half pray, "If only there was someone I could talk to...someone I could trust with my problems and decisions! Then I would know exactly what to do."

When your list of people comes up empty, you decide there isn't anyone who can help you. So you make your choice alone, with zero input from anybody else. Sometimes your choice is okay. But sometimes (like Megan's many bad choices) it leads to a train wreck.

The truth is, yes, there *is* someone you can trust 100 percent of the time, with 100 percent of the choices you have to make.

Now look again at Proverbs 3:5: *Trust in the LORD with all your heart*. Who does it say you should trust?

____

That someone is God, right? According to that same verse, how much are you to trust God?

____

God knows 100 percent of the time what is 100 percent best for you. He knows what is right for you, and exactly what you need—and don't need. He also knows what will be good or harmful for you. In fact, He is the best person you can count on for help with your choices!

You may already know all of this. But right now it is time for you to truly believe it and apply it in your life. In every choice you make, from the small ones to the giant ones, you must completely trust and believe that God can—and will—help you make the right choice. That's where *with all your heart* (verse 5) comes in.

God will help you make *really* good choices when you completely trust Him to help you and guide you.

Resist doing things on your own. *Lean not on your own understanding* (verse 5). If you were to lean against a wall, what would be supporting you?

____

God is not asking you to give up your ability to think and reason. But He is asking you to not lean on, or count on, or depend on your own wisdom. Do you know everything? Have you experienced everything there is to experience?

Your answer to each of these questions has got to be *no*. This is why God says you shouldn't try to lean on your own wisdom. Instead, you need to listen to the wisdom of God's Word, your parents, and wise teachers like Miss Julie.

This was Megan's problem. She wanted what she wanted. And she was listening to everyone but God. She was ignoring God and the truths in the Bible when she made her choices. Megan was definitely leaning on her own understanding!

You and every person on the planet will always be tempted to do something wrong. But here's a verse that gives you even more reason to trust God:

> *No temptation has overtaken you except what is common to mankind. And God is faithful; he will not let you be tempted beyond what you can bear. But when you are tempted, he will also provide a way out so that you can endure it* (1 Corinthians 10:13).

Jot down several truths this verse tells you about God:

____

____

____

____

____

Megan got into trouble because she failed to take the time to pray and ask God and her parents for help with the people, opportunities, and issues in her life. What will you do the next time you need to make a choice that you are not sure about?

____

____

____

Understand who is in control. *In all your ways acknowledge Him* (Proverbs 3:6 NASB)—How do you acknowledge the presence of a friend? You call out her name. You wave. You flash a smile and yell out a greeting. Maybe you run up to her and give her a big hug.

Acknowledging God is no different. What do these verses say about God's presence in your life?

Do not be afraid; do not be discouraged, for the LORD your God will be with you wherever you go (Joshua 1:9).

____

____

____

I [Jesus] *am with you always, to the very end of the age* (Matthew 28:20).

The Lord is always with you. He is always present, even though you cannot see Him. And He promises that He will never leave you or forsake you or turn on you. He does all this for you. Yet there is something you must do: You are to always acknowledge His presence in your life. According to the verses that follow, what is the best way to acknowledge God?

To you, LORD, I called; to the Lord I cried (Psalm 30:8).

Do not be anxious about anything, but in every situation, by prayer...present your requests [needs] *to God* (Philippians 4:6).

What are you *not* to do when you have a problem?

What are you to do instead?

____

____

Through prayer you can talk to God about every decision you must make. He will gladly help you with your choices. Every choice is important to Him...and should be to you too. So pray with a sincere heart, "Lord, what will You have me do? What is the right thing to do?"

Straight paths come with God's help. *And he will make your paths straight* (verse 6). Your part in making *really* good choices is to acknowledge God in everything and seek to do things His way. According to the verse quoted here, what does God promise He will do?

____

____

Some translations say, *He shall direct your paths* (NKJV). In other words, God's job is to direct and guide you—to make your path obvious and straight. He will clear the way for you so you can move onward to what is best for you and pleases Him. You will be making the right choices... which means you will be enjoying life more and making bad choices less. How cool is that?

Time to choose. Megan was listening to Miss Julie teach about Proverbs 3:5 and 6, and she found the help her heart was longing for! It was as if a light turned on. And it was so simple! All she had to do was trust God with the details of her life, and *God* would help her make *really* good choices—the right choices!

But there was just one little problem—Megan's sin. She had chalked up quite a long list of sins these past few weeks. Megan sighed and wondered, "How can I make a fresh start with God? Is there any way I can just start over? How can I get my life turned around?"

Then Megan wondered, "How could God ever forgive me?"

Well, God came to the rescue once again! And again, He used Miss Julie, who seemed to be reading Megan's mind as she read from Ephesians 1:7:

> *In him* [Jesus] *we have redemption through his blood, the forgiveness of sins, in accordance with the riches of God's grace.*

What happens to our sin when we put our faith and trust in Jesus?

____

____

God is 100 percent holy and sinless. On the other hand, all people are sinful. As a result, all people are separated from God. The *bad news* is that because of our sin, we deserve punishment and death. But the *good news* is that because of Jesus' death on a cross, we can accept by faith that Jesus died in our place for our sins. We can have forgiveness for our sins!

Then Miss Julie gave a simple prayer for any of the girls who had not received God's forgiveness of their sin. She encouraged them to pray this prayer. She also reminded them that the prayer must come from their heart and be sincere:

Jesus, I know I am a sinner. I want to turn from my sins and follow You. I believe You died for my sins and rose again, and I want to accept You as my personal Savior. Come into my life, Lord Jesus, and help me to obey You from now on. Amen.

Megan prayed along with Miss Julie because she knew in her heart that she needed to turn her life over to Jesus—to do it for real. As she finished the prayer, Megan knew without a doubt that she truly believed that Jesus was her Savior. She knew her sins had been forgiven now that she had committed her life to Jesus. And Megan knew something else—she really wanted to do what was right, to live God's way, to make *really* good choices.

What freedom! All Megan could do was thank God over and over in her heart for a fresh start—for a new heart! She felt clean from the past—and the past several weeks! In her heart, she was done with living for herself, and ready and excited to start *really* living for Jesus!

The Choice Is Yours

Ask yourself right now—today—these questions: Do I need to do what the verse in Proverbs says—to "trust in the LORD" with all my heart? Have I fully trusted God by giving my heart to Jesus? If you say you have, write down some choices you have made that show yourself, your family, and others that you are living for Jesus.

____

____

____

Are there ways I could be growing as a Christian? For instance, am I doing better at reading my Bible? Am I praying more often? Am I making progress at being a good family member, especially to Dad and Mom? What about my brother, my sister? Jot down some ideas you have that will help you grow stronger in these areas:

____

____

____

____

Making Really Good Choices

In this chapter we have looked into God's Word and learned about **T-R-U-S-T**. On this page, write out the point of each letter. (I'll get you started with "T.")

Trust in the Lord.

R ______________________________

U ______________________________

S ______________________________

T ______________________________

Now write out one thing you liked, learned, or want to do about trusting God.

____

____

____

____

____

____

Take time now to seal your desire to make *really* good choices with the words of this prayer:

> *Dear Lord, help me to remember that I can always lean on You. Whenever I have a problem, a concern, or a decision to make, I know I can trust You to guide me in making the right choice. I give You my heart, and I want to trust in You with all my heart. Amen.*

A Bestseller by Elizabeth George

A Girl After God's Own Heart

Homework! Friends! Activities! Parents! The life of a tween girl is full of so much action—and sometimes so much *confusion*! How can I find a real best friend? How can I get along with my brothers and sisters? How can I make time in my busy life for Jesus? How can I know the right things to say and do—especially when I keep messing up?

As you set out on this fun adventure with Jesus, you'll learn what it means to be a girl after God's own heart—a girl who loves Him and follows Him by...

- growing in love for your family and friends—even when it seems like you're all alone
- growing in wisdom as you learn to make good choices and fewer mistakes
- growing in grace as you face the things that are hard—from friendships, to schoolwork, to doubts about yourself
- growing in joy as you fall more and more in love with Jesus

Walking with God is the most amazing journey a girl can take. Start today! Take your first steps to becoming a girl after God's own heart.

Books by Elizabeth George for Teen Girls

A Young Woman After God's Own Heart

What does it mean to include God's heart in your everyday life? It means understanding and following His perfect plan for your friendships, your faith, your family relationships, and your future. Learn how to grow close to God, enjoy meaningful relationships, make wise choices, become spiritually strong, build a better future, and fulfill the desires of your heart.

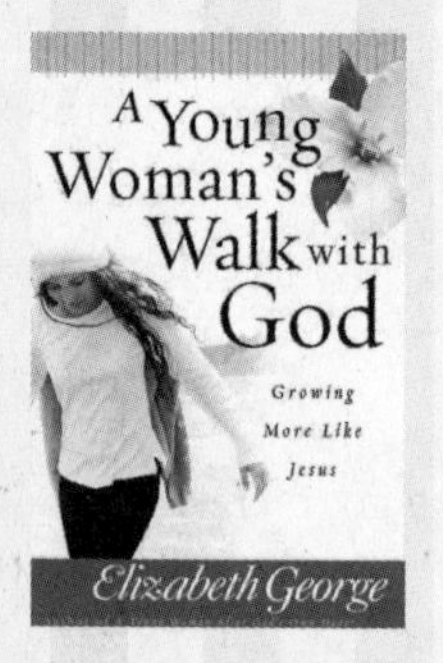

A Young Woman's Walk with God

Love, joy, peace, patience, kindness, goodness, faithfulness, gentleness, and self-control are qualities Jesus possessed—and He wants you to have them too! Elizabeth George takes you step-by-step through the fruit of the Spirit to help you get the most out of your life.

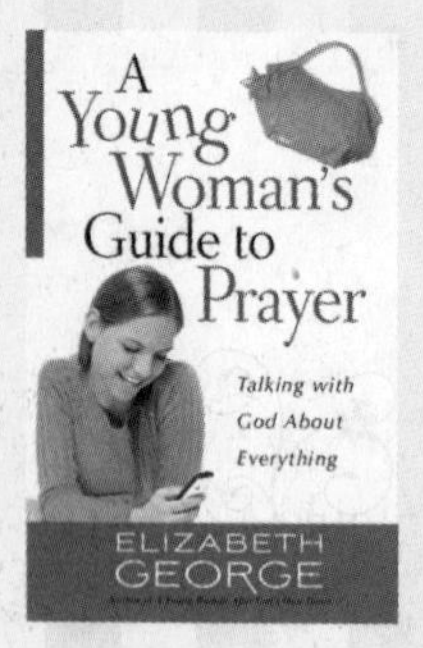

A Young Woman's Guide to Prayer

God has given you an amazing gift—the ability to talk with Him every day! Through prayer, you can share with God your joys and triumphs, hurts and fears, wants and needs. He cares about every detail of your life. God is your forever friend, and He's always ready to talk with you!

A Young Woman's Guide to Making Right Choices

When it comes to making decisions, how can you make sure you are making the right choices, the best choices? Do you desire to please God in the way you pick your friends, spend your time, and treat your family? You'll find useful checkpoints for helping you understand God's wisdom and living it out.

A Young Woman After God's Own Heart—A Devotional

God wants to encourage you each and every day! He has things to say to you that can change your day, take away your worries, and give you hope. In His amazing love, He cares about all the details of your life. In this pocket-sized devotional, you'll learn how to take your problems to God, let go of your worries, live your faith, find a real friend in Jesus, and grow in true beauty and confidence.